LIGHT TRUCK.

MILITARY FIRE FIGHTERS

MILITARY CONSTRUCTION TRUCKS

HEAVY-DUTY WRECKER

MARINE DIESEL ENGINES

AIRFIELD CRASH TRUCK

THUNDERBOLT

TANK MAINTENANCE & OPERATORS' SCHOOL

FIELD DYNAMOMETER TRUCK

PONTOON BRIDGE CARRIER

3/4 TRACK TRUCK

NAVY FUEL TRUCK

PRIME MOVER FOR "LONG TOM" GUN

CARGO CARRIER

AL SHERMAN TANK-TRANSMISSION

U.S. NAVY PERSONNEL TRANSPORT BUS

U.S. NAVY HELIUM-HAULER

ONE COMPANY'S PART...

No—we're not showing you how Mack is "winning the war." A swell lot of youngsters called Joe are doing that.

But we are proud of what Mack does *to help*. Every item shown here, and others we couldn't show, was once an engineering "headache." To make each possible, some knotty special problem of design or manufacture had to be whipped.

Working with America's splendid ordnance engineers, Mack engineers have cracked these tough nuts, one by one.

In doing the job—with us as with other companies who have put war needs ahead of all else—a big share of credit goes to our good Mack users here at home. Their peacetime equipment is doing a mighty wartime job.

Mack TRUCKS

ONE TON TO FORTY-FIVE TONS; BUSES, FIRE APPARATUS AND MARINE ENGINES

Mack Trucks, Inc., Empire State Bldg., New York, N. Y.

About the Author

Since World War II, when a youngster in German-occupied Holland, Bart Vanderveen has been involved in every aspect of the military vehicle scene — both historic and modern. He became fascinated by the vast array of automotive equipment, first of the Wehrmacht and in due course of the Allied liberators, and enthusiastically started collecting pictures, manuals and anything else in print on which he could lay his eager hands. In time he joined the armed forces' Technical Service for two years, gaining valuable hands-on experience with modern and old army motor transport and afterwards owned a succession of demobbed relics, from Jeep and Kübel to Command and Heavy Utility. Today a vast reference and photo library is one of the results of this hobby, which he has always been anxious to share with other enthusiasts. He had his first book published in 1969 and numerous other titles have followed, the best known being the Observer's *Fighting Vehicles Directory* and the *Historic Military Vehicles Directory.* He has been responsible for articles and contributions about military and other vehicles in many periodicals and books and on several occasions has appeared on radio and television. He has gained an international reputation for his knowledge on this specialist subject and is frequently consulted by both military and civil authorities. In 1982 he became freelance editor of *Wheels & Tracks,* the widely acclaimed international review of military vehicles, published by *After the Battle.*

A record of military
MACKs
in the Services and beyond

By Bart Vanderveen

AN
AFTER THE BATTLE
PUBLICATION

COLOPHON

A *Wheels & Tracks Directory*
© Bart Vanderveen 1998
Printed in Great Britain
ISBN: 1 870067 09 6
An *After the Battle* publication

PUBLISHERS

Battle of Britain International Ltd
Church House, Church Street, London E15 3JA
Telephone: 0181-534 8833
Fax: 0181-555 7567
E-mail: afterthebattle@mcmail.com

PRINTERS

Biddles Ltd
Guildford and King's Lynn

COVER

Well-known Mack faces from World Wars I and II and the Cold War: AC, NM, RD.

FRONTISPIECE

Mack NMs with Rogers trailers hauling new tanks in wartime Britain, 1944.

ENDPAPERS

Assorted Mack period advertisments from the 'teens, early 'forties (see also page 61) and more recently.

ACKNOWLEDGEMENTS

This work was compiled and written largely from historic source material in the author's collection, including original Mack literature (manuals, parts lists, specifications) and pictures plus numerous items from other official sources and private collections. The following Mack aficionados deserve special mention for assistance and generously donating valuable material over many years: Jim Bibb, Colin Chisholm (the late curator of the Mack Museum), Fred Crismon, Martien Monné, John Montville (author of several Mack books) and Davide Virdis.

DEDICATION

To the memory of W. Colin Chisholm (1919-1997).

CONTENTS

Introduction	6
The Teens and Twenties	
4×2	8
6×2	16
6×4	17
Tracks	18
The Thirties and Forties	
4×2	20
4×4	41
6×4	43
6×6	69
8×8	92
Tracks	94
Post-World War II	
4×2	99
6×4	102
6×6	109
8×8	126
Surplus: Army Macks in mufti	
4×2, 4×4	130
6×4	132
6×6	139
Colourful Macks: Preservation	
General	153
4×2	154
6×4	155
6×6	157
Index	160

was universally known as the 'Bulldog' — reached a total of more than 40,000, with frequent upgrading and in many variants, until the late 1930s.

The first Mack for military use was supplied in 1911 to the US War Department. It was a 1-ton truck, with serial number (s/n) 1198 and fitted with a 'regular army style' body, to be used as a demonstrator. Shipment, to Washington, DC, took place on October 20, and in Army records it

Left: One of the first Mack Jr 1½-tonners of the USMC, this being s/n 2621 which operated at the Brooklyn, NY, Navy Yard and Marine Barracks, from 1913. Engine was 4-cyl. with 4½x5½ in. bore and stroke.
Below: Mack Sr 3-ton truck on 156-in. wheelbase chassis with 36x5 front and 42x4 (dual) rear tyres. Body was dark blue with grey striping and features 'swinging gates' on either side. Engine was 5½x6-in. L-head Four, final drive by side chains. It was delivered in 1912.

Introduction

Mack is one of the world's oldest surviving vehicle marques. The company began as a wagon-building enterprise in Brooklyn, NY, and in 1905 acquired a factory in Allentown, PA, which is still the location of the main plant. By 1911/12, Mack joined forces with American Saurer and Hewitt, the group being named the International Motor Company. The Mack name, however, soon supplanted the others.

Early models were of the cab-over-engine configuration, followed by the successful Junior (1- to 2-ton) and Senior (up to 7½-ton) models. During 1914-16, new designs were worked out by Edward R. Hewitt, then the Chief Engineer. These were the famed AB and AC model ranges. The AC — which

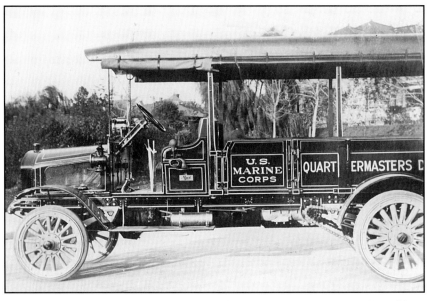

shows up as a 1½-tonner. By June 30, 1915, it had run 3,308 miles and hauled 376 tons of cargo. Cost of operation thus far had been $218.79, plus $720 'chauffeur wages, including rations and clothing'. Tyre expenses had totalled $116.38 and an indication of the vehicle's quality was that the 'Time laid up' was zero! During the next 12 months it ran another 1,170 miles, hauling 390 tons.

The US Army's next Mack trucks were s/n 2970 and 2971: 1½-tonners for use in El Paso, TX. These were shipped on June 6, 1914 and by mid-1915 had covered in excess of 6,000 miles each with no problems to speak of. Meanwhile, the Marine Corps had invested in half a dozen, as follows:

Serial	Model	Date of Delivery
1990	3-ton Sr	June 11, 1912
2538	1½-ton Jr	March 27, 1913
2621	1½-ton Jr	May 20, 1913
2677	2-ton Jr	July 1, 1913
2683	1½-ton Jr	July 22, 1913
3211	3-ton Sr	Nov. 11, 1913

Mack AC — alias Bulldog — 3½- and 5½-ton chassis/cabs for the AEF in Europe, 1918.

World War II: Convoy of Mack NM-series 6-ton 6x6 trucks, serving the British Army as Medium Artillery Tractors, ready for action.

The first four were used at USMC facilities in Philadelphia, PA; Norfolk, VA; and Brooklyn, NY; the last two on the Pacific islands of Guam and Honolulu respectively.

In 1915 the company produced several experimental prototypes expressly for military use. These were made available for field trials by the National Guard during the Plattsburg Military Maneuvers in the summer of that year. Two were armoured. This event was also the debut of the impressive AC in its military role. In 1916 came the first military order: 150 for the British Army. It was the British who dubbed them Bulldogs. When the US got directly involved in the Great War in April 1917 many more Bulldogs appeared in military livery: More than 1,300 saw service with the AEF in France during 1917-18 and after the Armistice many were surplussed, remaining in Europe serving civilian owners well into the 1930s, and longer.

In the 1920s and '30s few Macks were newly ordered for the armed forces but by 1940 this changed again, and dramatically. Again it was at first mainly for Europe but when the United States entered World War II virtually the whole production of Mack and other vehicle producers was for Uncle Sam and the Allies, with thousands of vehicles being supplied for Defence Aid under the Lend-Lease arrangement which was enacted in March 1941.

During 1940-45 Mack Manufacturing Corp. supplied well over 32,000 vehicles for military purposes. Half of these were NR-series 6x4 trucks with diesel engine. Second in quantity was the NM 6-ton 6x6 range. By far the majority of these Macks were shipped overseas. Afterwards many were remanufactured for another lease of life, thereby often losing their original identity.

In monetary terms, the total of all Mack military sales (including trucks, trailers, tank transmissions, spare parts, diesel engines, plant facilities, etc.) up to December 31, 1944, amounted to $292,424,584.40, reaching well over 300 million dollars by the time that the war was over.

In the post-WWII period relatively few new Macks were supplied for military service. Most were one-offs or small groups of militarized commercial trucks, invariably premium types, custom-built and with price tags to match. The main exceptions — in terms of numbers — were the M-series 6x6 trucks which Mack produced (to government design) in the 5- and 10-ton classes; a fleet of 6x4 refuellers in the early 1980s and the Australian jobs. Most if not all are presented in this book.

Meanwhile, during the 1950s and '60s Mack had expanded considerably and taken over other truck builders: Brockway in the US (1956), Bernard in France (1963) and Hayes in Canada (1969). In the late 1970s Renault Véhicules Industriels (Renault V.I. or RVI), in turn, took an interest in Mack and the Allentown company became a division of the French concern. Light and medium Macks became badge-engineered Renaults and some were supplied to the military, but of greater importance to Renault was Mack's E9 V8 16.4-litre diesel engine which comes in several versions, for truck and AFV applications. The most powerful variant developed 750 bhp and in the future probably up to 1000 bhp (736 kW).

Early 1980s: Chassis/cabs (Model DM492S) for refuelling units for the US Air Force.

Mack AB   Truck, 2-ton, 4x2   1915

GENERAL

Launched in 1914 the AB 'Baby Mack' remained in production with periodic detail improvements and upgrading until the mid-1930s during which time more than 55,000 were built. In 1915 the makers loaned a pair of AB models to the New York State National Guard at Plattsburg, NY, for military manoeuvres in August, one with chain-drive, the other with shaft-drive to the rear wheels, both with optional pneumatic tyres. They were described at the time as Engineering Development Vehicles, hence the numbers E-3 and E-4 displayed on them. The latter had a lowered silhouette and looked quite sporty. They may have been the only 'military' AB trucks ever.

PHYSICAL

AB-type Macks were of contemporary conventional design. The open cabs had a folding canvas top. Side curtains could be installed. Wheelbase of the standard model measured 146.5 in., overall width (over the rear wheel hubs) 75 in. Track width was 58 in. front, 60 in. rear.

TECHNICAL

Specification shows bore and stroke of 4.25 x 5 in. and 283.7 cubic inches displacement for the 34-bhp L-head engine. The crankshaft had three main bearings. Carburettor was a 1.5-in. Stromberg OT2, magneto a Splitdorf SS4. The 33-gal. fuel tank was normally placed under the seat. Engine oil capacity was 3 gal., the cooling system held 6.25 gal. Drive line comprised 3-speed gearbox and worm- or chain-drive rear axle. Tyres were normally 36-in. solids but the subject vehicles had the optional pneumatics, 36x6 front and 40x8 rear.

Top: Chain-drive transport truck E-4 with low silhouette (notice fuel tank outside frame).

Above: E-3 was of more conventional configuration.

Bottom: Typical AB shaft-drive chassis.

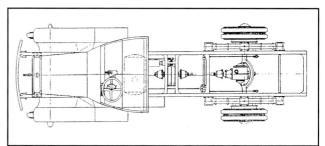

Mack AB   Armoured Car   1915/16

GENERAL

On April 6, 1916, *The Automobile* reported: 'An Armored Motor Truck Battery, with a quota of 160 men and six officers, was formally mustered into the New York State National Guard. For its equipment four experimental armored cars were prepared'. It was a private venture and they were among America's first. This example, built on a 1915 Mack AB 2-ton truck chassis was one of them. It was armed with two 'rapid-fire guns' (MGs) on fixed tripods. A second model was different in detail and a couple more were produced on Locomobile and White chassis. The Mack's armour (and probably that of the others, too) was made of 'special heat-treated steel of great hardness and resists regulation US Army rifle or machine gun fire at 50 yd.'

PHYSICAL

The AB-based armoured cars had an open-top hull of bolted armour plates and a rear access door. It measured 212 by 76.5 in. and stood 65 in. tall (excluding armament). Weight was just over 9,000 lb. The wooden spoked wheels were protected by steel discs. The radiator protection was different on the two vehicles. At the rear of the vehicle was a spring-cushioned towing eye.

TECHNICAL

Mack's own 284-cid (4.25 x 5 in.) 4-cyl. side-valve (L-head) engine of 34 bhp drove the rear wheels via a 3-speed gearbox and worm-drive differential. Fuel feed was by Stewart vacuum system. Electrics included engine starting and lighting (incl. a 10-in. Gray & Davis searchlight). The wheels had solid rubber-block 36-in. tyres, dual rear. Steering gear was of the cam-lever type and could be controlled also from the rear.

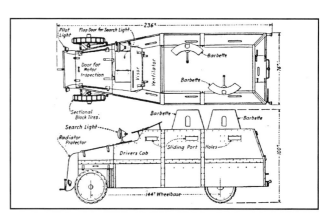

Top: Original version, seen in 1916.

Above: Pre-production plan and side elevation drawings.

Below: Second version, with revised front and shown minus armament.

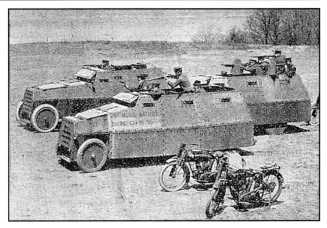

Top: The second version of the armoured car on Mack AB chassis had four horizontal cooling slots in addition to the large air scoop below. Middle: Of this trio (on its way to Peekskill, June 29, 1916) the centre one is the original Mack. Its front armour was later modified, too. Bottom: The 'Armored Motor Car Section' in training in 1917.

Mack AC   Truck, 3½-ton, 4x2   1917/18

GENERAL

In 1914 plans were laid for a new heavy-duty Mack truck, supplanting the dated Sr (Senior) design. Prototypes were produced and tested and in March 1916 the new AC range was launched at the Boston Truck Show. There were several payload classes. In early 1917 the British WD (which already had an earlier 3-tonner with 5½x6-in. 48.4 HP engine) ordered a fleet of 150 ACs for military use. All of these survived the war. The name Bulldog was reportedly first applied by a British WD engineer; it was soon adopted by Mack. The US Army Quartermaster Corps procured 368, of which 278 were shipped to the AEF in France. They were officially known as Truck, 3-5 ton, Cargo (Mack); Symbol HC3. The heavier 5½-ton types (see following entry) were more numerous.

Top: 'Cargo B' truck (symbol HC3) in France.

Above: Chassis/cab ready for delivery in Allentown, 1918.

Below: US 46405 with different (non-standard) cargo body.

PHYSICAL

The AC model had an exceptionally sturdy chassis, with the radiator mounted behind the engine. The largely open steel cab had a cantilever-type roof. The US Army's had 168-in. wheelbase and were mostly fitted with a wooden cargo body. Chassis/cab dimensions were 265 x 87 x 100 in. approx.; standard B cargo body measured 152 x 86 x 31 (w/bows 80) in. Weight, chassis/cab, 8,070 lb, body 1,600 lb.

TECHNICAL

Own 471-cid (5x6 in.) 4-cyl. L-head engine of 40 HP SAE rating (actual power output 70+ bhp at 1,000 rpm), driving the rear axle via a 3-speed gearbox, combined with differential and jackshaft, and chains. Reduction 13.42:1. HT magneto ignition. Solid rubber tyres, 36x5 front, 40x5 dual rear, on wooden spoke wheels.

11

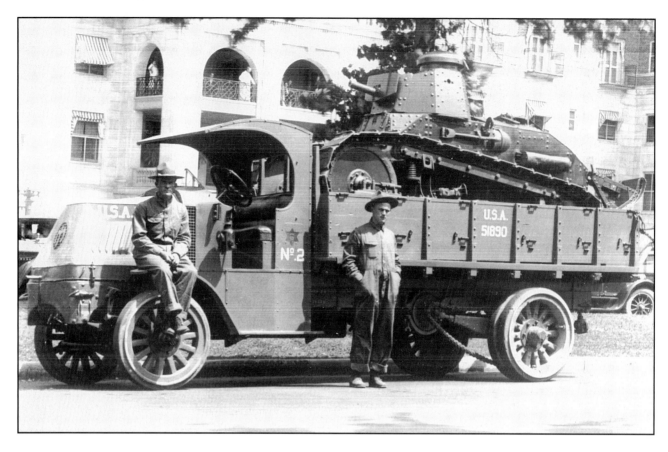

Mack AC   Truck, 5½-ton, 4x2   1917/18

GENERAL

Next size up from the 3½-ton Bulldog was the Truck, 5½-ton, Cargo; Symbol EHC1. They were more numerous: the US Army alone, in 1917, ordered a total of 5,575, of which 2,563 had been completed by November 1, 1918, when contracts were terminated. 1,365 had been 'floated overseas'. The British Army's 150 were also of the 5½-ton type; these were all listed as present in the UK in 1919. Most of the US Army's 5½-tonners were operated by the Corps of Engineers: Repair trucks, Symbol R1 (Blacksmith), R2 (Carpenter), R3 (Machine Shop), R5 (Material); Special Operating trucks S5 (Laboratory Sterilizer), S6 (Lithographic), S8 (Printing Press); Tank trucks TK3 (Sprinkler, Water). There were also a short-wheelbase Dump truck (EHD1) and a wrecker. The letters EH in the model symbols stood for Extra Heavy.

PHYSICAL

The 5½-ton model was similar to the 3½-tonner but the chassis frame and road springs were stronger and the rear tyres wider. Wheelbase was 168 in. except for the dump truck which had the shorter 156-in. wheelbase chassis. The steel dump body measured 147 x 84 x 29 in. and had a hydraulic hoist. The shop trucks had a fixed-top van-type body with opening side(s).

TECHNICAL

Same engine and gearbox (1-3: 2.825, 1.725 and 1.00:1; reverse 3.767:1) as the 3½-ton model. Tyres were 36x5 front and 40x6 dual rear. Dump truck had Wood hydraulic hoist, driven from gearbox PTO. All Bulldogs had a pressed steel frame with a bolted front cross member to facilitate engine removal.

Top: Cargo truck (with Standardized B body) carrying M1917 Light Tank (French Renault FT, US-built under licence).

Above: 1,200-gallon Tanker with sprinkler (TK3).

Below: Dump truck on SWB chassis (EHD1)

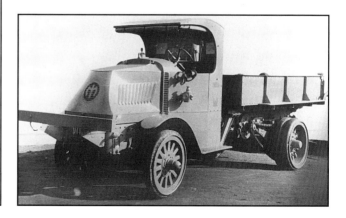

Top: Blacksmith shop van (R1) in travelling mode and, on the right, the relatively rare short-wheelbase (156-in.) wrecker.
Middle: One of the fixed-roof shop trucks was the Lithographic (S6) outfit seen here at work. The equipment was hand-power operated. Body measured 156 x 78 x 72 in. Left-hand side was fixed and had windows; other side opened. Door at rear.
Bottom: Tank and Dump trucks on a road building project by the 23rd US Army Engineers in France.

AC Bulldog Miscellany

Top: Pilot model as loaned to the US Army Reserve towing a 3-in. field gun for the New York National Guard from New York City to Plattsburg in 1915, and, right, a militarised AC as cargo truck with folding-top cab, special front bumper and other unusual features, 1917.
Above: A rather peculiar military variant of the famed Bulldog was this searchlight

truck of the early 1920s. Its chassis was extended at the front to carry an engine-driven generator that provided electric current. The sprung bumper was fitted to many military Bulldogs. The searchlight truck had two radiators to cool the engine during stationary use. The searchlight was a 40-in. mirror type of 1,000,000 candle power.

Below left: A Light Tank, T1E1 (Cunningham, 1928) mounting a 1920s' AC '4-speeder' (i.e. with 4-speed transmission), probably civilian, and, *below right,* another, lighter, searchlight carrier, with crew seats, pneumatic tyres and cable reel at rear. The searchlight was of the parabolic-reflector type, but no other details seem to have survived.

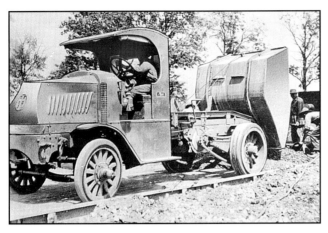

After WWI ex-Army and new Bulldogs were a familiar sight, both Stateside (here with skip and as tractor-trailer) and abroad.

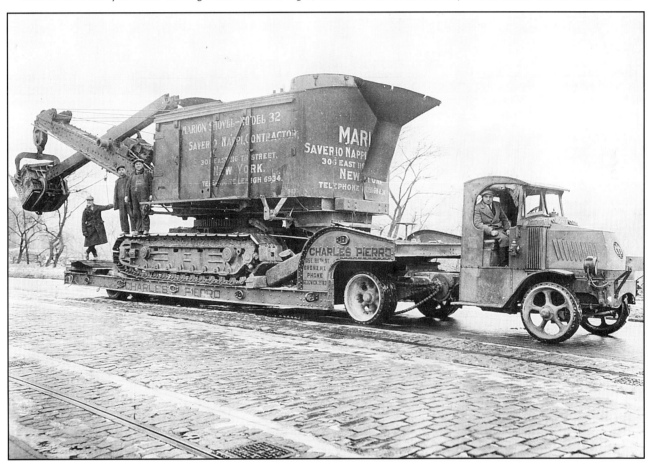

1920s' civilian 4-speed tractor with 28-ton low-loading semi-trailer carrying a Marion shovel of 95,500 lb. (nearly 43 metric tons).

Whether civvy (left) or demobbed ex-military (right), the Bulldog's characteristic appearance boosted Mack's international image.

AC Six-wheelers

In 1926 Mack offered a 6x2 Super-Duty chassis with 'tag axle', to be followed by the 6x4 AP in 1929 (*qv*). The 6x2 had inverted semi-elliptic leaf springs on both bogie axles. Christie designed tracks which could be hung under the body when not in use.

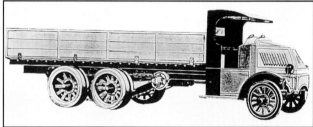

Mack AP   Truck, 8-ton, 6x4, Prime Mover, T2   1929

GENERAL

In 1926 a new 6-cylinder engine, the 150-bhp Model AP, was introduced for extra heavy-duty applications of the Bulldog chassis, e.g. the Type 15 fire apparatus with 1000-gpm pump. A new six-wheeled chassis with this new engine was also developed and, like the engine, designated Model AP. In 1929 the US Army Ordnance Department procured some of these trucks for prime mover and tank-hauling duties, with a payload rating of 8 tons. Of the former, four were standardised as Anti-aircraft tractors, M2. The price of the (commercial) AP 10-ton 6x4 was $12,000, twice that of a 7½ -ton 4x2 Model AC. The AC (with 4-cyl. engine) was also available in six-wheeler form, at $7,500.

PHYSICAL

The AP had a longer hood than the AC and Ordnance specified enclosed cabs with sliding doors, front bumper, steel bodies and other special features like a winch on some models. Pneumatic tyres gave the truck a more modern appearance. Overall dimensions were 336 x 109 x 96 in., wheelbase 222 (BC 52) in. The vehicle weighed in at 22,380 lb and the GVW was 42,380 lb.

TECHNICAL

Mack's 6-cyl. L-head AP engine had 5 x 6-in. bore and stroke dimensions providing 707 cubic inches displacement and it developed 124 bhp net (150 gross) at 2,000 rpm. All rear wheels were chain-driven via a 4-speed gearbox. Tyres were size 40x8 all round. Maximum speed was 20 mph.

Top: Tank carrier hauling Light Tank, T1E1.

Above: Tank carrier with trailer.

Below: Artillery tractor (without winch).

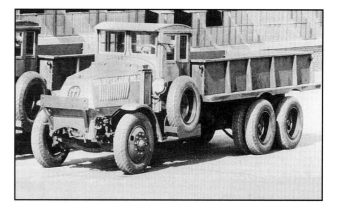

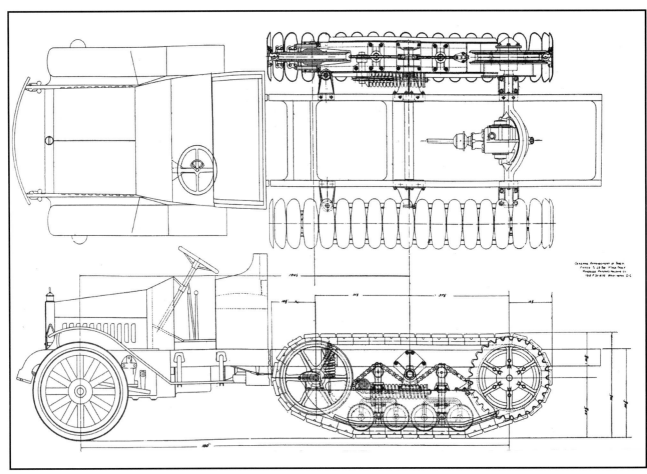

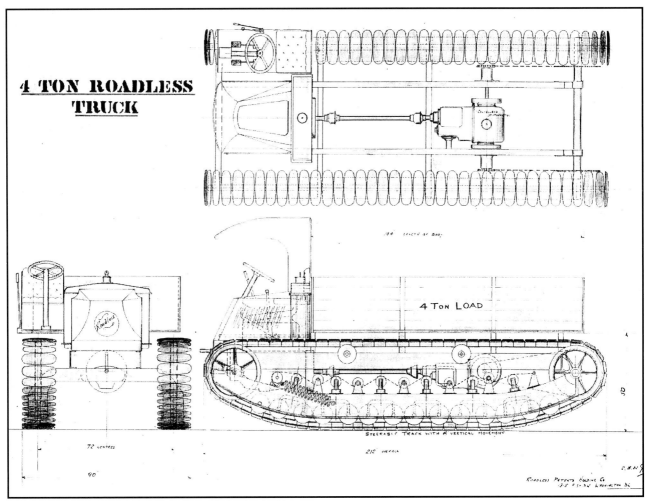

4 TON ROADLESS TRUCK

4 TON LOAD

Tracks for Macks from Christie and Roadless

In the early 1920s Roadless Traction Limited of Hounslow, Middlesex, in association with a US subsidiary Roadless Patent Holdings in Washington, DC, experimented with new track-laying systems and designed a half-track conversion for the Mack AB (of which a prototype was constructed and tested) and a 4-ton full-track carrier version (on paper only) of the AC Bulldog truck. Both are shown opposite. They featured universally jointed track shoes and a suspension system whereby a wire rope or chain arrangement provided equal downward pressure on all bogie rollers. More numerous were the track conversions by John Walter Christie.

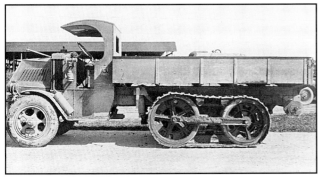

Christie Crawlers, Inc. of Newark, NJ, offered various half-track systems, from simple overall chains for standard tandem bogies (shown on a civilian Mack AB, top; see also page 16) to

complete bogies incorporating the truck's existing drive axle and wheels. The latter were known as the Christie Crawler Attachment. One such conversion — of a 1917 Mack AC

5½-tonner — was tested around 1923 by the US Army Ordnance Dept, as shown in the middle pictures. The final photo portrays a later development, featuring better weight distribution on the track.

Mack DE   Truck, 1½-ton, 4x2, Cargo   1939

GENERAL

In the period 1939-41 most US truck manufacturers received Government orders for commercial trucks, some of which were militarised to a certain extent. The heading photo shows a typical example, a Mack DE of the US Navy. It was, in fact, assigned by the Navy Department to the training ship USS *Prairie State,* which was permanently moored to a dock in the Hudson River in New York City. These DE trucks (1939-42) were among the lightest Macks ever built and in their basic standard form had 136.5-in. wheelbase and 6.00-20 tyres, single all round. Longer wheelbase sizes, larger tyres and dual rear were all optional. It was one size up from the ED (1938-44) which as standard had 120.5-in. wheelbase and 6.00-17 tyres. They were often called Baby Macks — like the old AB models — and certainly the little ED was 'the most overbuilt truck ever sold in the light-duty field'.

PHYSICAL

Conventional commercial truck with factory-supplied 2-seat steel cab. Wheelbase 152.5 in. Composite steel and wood body with fixed front and roof and roll-up canvas curtains at sides and rear. Overall dimensions approx. 240 x 75 in. Height over cab 81 in.

TECHNICAL

Continental EN11 210-cid L-head Six engine, 67 bhp at 3,000 rpm. 4-speed constant-mesh gearbox. Full-floating rear axle. Hydraulic brakes. Open spider-type wheels with six cast spokes and 7.00-20 tyres, dual rear.

Top: USN cargo/general duty truck (USN 11943).

Above: GS truck with RHD and open cab of Portuguese Army in Mozambique (QG189). (The Portuguese forces also had heavier E-series trucks.)

Below: Typical application of DE chassis with single rear tyres.

Mack EE(S)   Truck, 2½-ton, 4x2, Dump   1940

GENERAL

In 1939 the US Army ordered 80 Mack EES dump trucks under QMC Contract 7452. Delivered in 1940 they were registered USA W-410794-873. Purchase price was $1,665 each but in 1944 the War Department valued them at $1,782 each. Basically a commercial EE truck, the suffix S indicated special equipment like the U-profile front bumper and a 290-cid (vs 271-cid) engine. The official purpose description was 'to haul and dump earth, sand, gravel, coal, etc.'. The US Marine Corps had a fleet of similar dump (and other) trucks on the standard EE chassis/cab. EE model trucks of various types were also operated by the US Marine Corps, Navy and Coast Guard, some examples being shown here and on the following page.

PHYSICAL

Conventional chassis/cab with all-steel rear-tipping dump body, hydraulically-actuated. Spare wheel mounted behind the cab. Wheelbase 144.5 in. Overall length, width and height 218 x 91 x 85 in. Weight 8,450 lb, gross 13,450 lb. Two tow hooks at front.

TECHNICAL

Continental FK (Mack EN290) 290-cid 6-cyl. L-head engine, developing 92 bhp at 2,800 rpm and 200 lb.ft of torque at 1,200 rpm. 12-Volt electrics. Fuller 5A33 5-speed direct-top gearbox and 6.85:1 rear axle. Hydraulic brakes. Cast-spoke wheels with 8.25-20 tyres.

Top: Model EES dump truck of US Army (USA W-410813).

Above: Model EE dump truck of US Marine Corps (USMC 1315).

Below: Line-up of chassis/cabs for USMC at the factory.

21

Right: The US Navy had a fleet of refuellers and bulk fuel tankers on EE and EH chassis/cabs. This is an EE-based tanker, delivered in 1940. The fuel trucks were used at US Navy airfields. Macks of various types were a familiar sight at the Navy Department's yards and bases. Mack also supplied the US Navy with diesel marine engines for armoured surf-landing boats 'designed to make quick landings on hostile shores', as well as 'fire apparatus for dependable protection of the fabulously valuable Navy Yards', to quote from an interesting Mack brochure describing military products issued in late 1941.

Above: The US Coast Guard became a part of the Navy and also operated a number of Mack trucks, exemplified by the integral van which was employed for carrying radio equipment for use during floods and hurricane disasters and also for maintenance of radio apparatus at USCG stations. The stake rack/cargo truck was used — also by the Coast Guard — as a personnel and equipment carrier and towed a trailer-mounted surf boat. Notice the power winch in the front of the body.

Left: The US Marine Corps also had several types of Macks, including this van-bodied unit of the Corps' Machine Shop in Philadelphia, PA. It was numbered USMC 1297 and the photo was taken on January 23, 1940.

Mack EF and EG   Truck, 2½-ton, 4x2, Chassis   1940

GENERAL

Prior to the acquisition of a batch of tank trucks on EHS chassis the US Army procured a pilot model on the lighter EF chassis. Carrying USA registration W-80235 it had a 1,000-gal. tank with side cabinets and catwalks. Of the slightly heavier contemporary EG model the Government purchased three dozen for Army service: 21 Dump, 12 Cargo and three Combination Stake and Platform (CS&P). The registrations were: Dump W-413728-735 and 741-751; Cargo W-413752-763; CS&P W-413736, 737 and 764. In 1944 they were listed as having values of $1,815, $1,801 and $1,742 respectively. As with other Mack commercial trucks and buses there were numerous options in respect of engines, transmissions, axles, tyres, wheelbases and there were COE models available also. The bus chassis variants included the following National Standard School Bus types (with related truck chassis model in brackets): SD (DE), SE (EE), SF (EF), SG (EG) and SH (EH), with wheelbase lengths from 136.5 to 266 in. In addition there were conventional type bus chassis (CBE, etc.) and rear-engined transit types (KB, etc.).

PHYSICAL

Similar in appearance to the EE models, the EF and EG were look-alikes, the differences being under-the-skin details. The next size up (EH) had different styling (see following pages).

TECHNICAL

(Model EG) Continental FK (Mack EN290) 6-cyl. L-head engine, 290 cid, 88 bhp at 2,750 rpm. Own TR30 5-speed direct-top gearbox. Timken 7.4:1 rear axle. Lockheed hydraulic service brakes. 8.25-20 tyres on cast-spoke wheels.

Top: Model EG chassis/cab for cargo and CS&P body.

Above: EF tanker (USA W-80235).

Below: US Navy bus on E-series chassis.

Mack EH series

EH
5-ton, 4x2, Fuel Servicing
1940

From the EH model upward, the Mack E series had a different hood and a V-shape radiator grille instead of the rounded type of the lighter models. The standard cab was basically the same but with a deeper cowl. The stylish design had been introduced in 1936, replacing the AB range. Shown is one of a number of aircraft refuellers of the US Navy, this one registered USN 7114. It carried 1,500 gal. of fuel and 100 gal. of lubricating oil. Equipment included chrome-plated assist rails, catwalks, fire extinguishers. Notice also the grounding chain at the rear. Power unit was Mack's own EN310 with up to 103 bhp. Coleman offered a 4WD conversion for the EH chassis.

EHS
5-ton, 4x2, Tank
1940

Registered USA W-80237 this was the second of a dozen 1,000-gal. bulk fuel and water tankers supplied to four QMC orders. Contract 7661 covered two fuel tankers (W-80236 and 237; 1940); Contract 8012 was for one ditto (W-80288); Contract 8297 was for a third (W-80290), still in 1940. There followed five water tankers (W-80752-755 and 758) and three water sprinklers (W-80756, 757, 759), all eight under Contract 8921 and delivered in early 1941. These trucks had a 176-in. wheelbase and rode on 9.00-20 tyres. Prices ranged from $3,500 to $3,800 approximately. Note the military style front bumper and towing hooks.

EHT
5-ton, 4x2, Tractor
1941

On June 16, 1941, the Quartermaster Corps on behalf of the British Government placed a special order for a fleet of 50 EH-series tractor trucks for shipment to the Far East. The contract was numbered DA-W-398-QM-16 (DA indicating Defense Aid). The vehicles (s/n EHT1D1960-2009) were shipped during the same year, along with 50 matching 8-ton 2-wheel Combination Stake and Platform semi-trailers which were also manufactured by Mack. The EHT had 141-in. wheelbase and 9.00-20 tyres. Normally the EN310 engine was fitted but the 112-bhp EN354 was optional, as was the Buda 6DT389 diesel. The subject tractors had the EN-354.

EHUS
4-ton, 4x2, Chassis
1940

Contract W-398-QM-7851 of April 16, 1940, was for two Mack truck chassis/cabs for the mounting of van bodies. The 162-in. WB COE chassis was selected. It cost $2,592, including $195 for the DeLuxe 195 model cab. (A hot-water type heater and a defroster for same cost another 16 and 5 dollars resp.) The military rated the completed vehicle at 2½-ton. A shorter version of this chassis was supplied under Contract 7672, also in 1940, for a single 4-ton tractor truck, designated EHUT. These tractor units were available with 108- or 132-in. wheelbase and could be fitted with the Buda 6DT389 diesel engine if required.

EHU
5-ton, 4x2, Wrecker
1940

Ordered in 1939 this Mack Model EHU COE (cab-over-engine) chassis/cab was shipped to the Ernest Holmes Co. in Chattanooga, TN, for the installation of a typical Holmes W35 double-boom wrecker unit with appropriate bodywork. The end product was destined for the US Marine Corps. The crane was power-operated from a PTO on the transmission except for the height adjustment of the booms which was a manual operation for which the hinged panels in the body sides had to be lowered. The front mudguards/fenders were unusual for these Macks in that they were of flat rather than curved section (and therefore of heavier-gauge steel than normal).

EMUT
5-ton, 4x2, Tractor
1942

In 1942 the QMC ordered 53 tractor trucks for semi-trailers from Mack under Contract 13116. (After August, when Ordnance took over responsibility for all the US Army's automotive procurement the contract code was changed to 670-3346.) The trucks were numbered USA 544345-397. The wheelbase measured 132 in. and the unit cost was a little over $3,000. In 1944 they were valued at $2,719. Standard engine of the EMUT was Mack's own EN354 of 112 bhp, but a diesel was optional. Outwardly similar to the EHUT the model shown is still minus its fifth-wheel coupling and quarter rear fenders/mudguards.

Mack EH   Truck, 5-ton, 4x2, Cargo   1942

GENERAL

510 of these militarised commercial trucks were built for Defense Aid. The QMC Contract was 12933 of May 22, 1942; Ordnance later changed it to W670-ORD-3339 (Oct. 30, 1942). There were several production lots and the chassis were numbered EH1S2637-2831 and 2833-3072, followed by EH1D3869-3943. US Army numbers were within the range 525499-526398. The trucks were supplied under Lend-Lease to Britain, along with COE models, incl. tractors, under Contract S/M 2765 and registered in the WD range L4952134-858. Confusingly all these trucks were variously referred to as 3-, 3½-, 4-, 5- and 6-ton in different American and British publications. Mack called them 5-tonners. See also following entries.

PHYSICAL

Devoid of brightwork and nameplates, mounting a military style cargo body with canvas cover and painted olive drab all over these trucks were further modified in Britain, as the lower picture shows: small single headlamp with BO mask, right-hand mirror, bridge plate, camouflage paint. Overall dimensions were 247 x 96 x 114 in., the body measured 126 x 84 in. Wheelbase 158 in. Weight 9,300 lb, GVW 16,900 lb.

TECHNICAL

All except 20 trucks had the Mack EN310 (310-cid) engine with TR30 5-speed gearbox (with either direct or overdrive top). The 20 exceptions had the larger EN354 engine, with Duplex (i.e. dual-range) 10-speed TRD31. Rear axles were also a mixture: RA36 on most, RA44 (dual reduction) on the last 75. All had hydraulic brakes.

Top: Early-production vehicle (s/n EH1S2695) as delivered, May 1942.

Above: Chassis/cab.

Below: L4952155 ready for service in the UK, November 1942.

Mack EHU   Truck, 5-ton, 4x2, Cargo   1942

GENERAL

Second in the mixed batch of EH-series Macks delivered in 1942 for Defense Aid was the Model EHU, the U indicating cab-over-engine (COE) or forward-control. The military received 70 of this particular type, with chassis s/n EHU1D1425-1494. The trucks were acquired under QMC Contract 12933 and delivered in two lots, with USA registrations W-525694-743 (50) and W-525861 (20). Like the conventional/-normal control Model EH (preceding entry) the trucks were shipped during the same year under Lend-Lease to Great Britain (Contract S/M 2765) where they received WD numbers from the range L4952134-858 and where minor alterations were made to lighting and other details to meet British WD requirements.

Top: First of the batch (s/n EHU1D1425) in June 1942.

Above and *below:* L4952300 readied for British service, December 1942.

PHYSICAL

Essentially a commercial COE truck this model was militarised to some extent by having OD paint, no brightwork or nameplates, army style cargo body with hoops and canvas tilt. Wheelbase was 144 in. first, 162 in. later. Body floor of the British truck shown measured 168 x 84 in. (inside) and overall length was 264 in. Weight 10,080 lb., gross 17,700 lb.

TECHNICAL

Own EN310 6-cyl. L-head engine, 100 bhp at 2,850 rpm. TR30 'Overgear' transmission (5-speed, overdrive top). RA44 dual reduction rear axle. Hydraulic brakes. Tyres 9.00-20. 6-Volt electrical equipment.

Mack EHT   Truck, 5-ton, 4x2, Tractor   1942

GENERAL

The mixed fleet of QMC Defence Aid Contract 12933 included 140 tractor trucks for semi-trailers, the latter also supplied by Mack (see page 30), all in 1942. Again the Lend-Lease recipient was Great Britain, where they arrived during the same year. Chassis Nos. ran from EHT1D2273-2302 and 2303-2412, the first batch having a dual-range transmission. US Army Nos. were in the range W-526156-295. The British contract number was Supply Mechanical (S/M) 2765 and the combination (tractor plus semi-trailer, in the UK often called 'artic') was known officially as 'Mack 6-ton 4x2-2 semi-trailer GS'. They were numbered within the WD Nos range L4952134-858.

PHYSICAL

EHTs were available (commercially) with 141- and 164-in. wheelbase, the latter for use with sleeper cab. The standard unit presented here (with 141-in WB) was fitted by the manufacturer with fifth-wheel coupling, pick-up plate, diamondette plate, quarter rear fenders and Model 195 DeLuxe type cab, to use all Mack nomenclature. Overall dimensions, including the semi-trailer, were 372 x 96 x 120 in. Weight 13,550 lb.

TECHNICAL

EN354 112-bhp 6-cyl. L-head engine with TR31 overdrive-top 5-speed gearbox except on first 30 vehicles which had TRD310D Duplex Overgear, i.e. two ranges, from 9.17 to 0.79:1. Rear axle RA44, dual-reduction. Air-operated brakes. 9.00-20 tyres. 6-Volt electrics.

Top and *above:* First of the second batch, s/n EHT1D2303, new and unmarked, June 1942.

Below: H4952849 in Britain, later in 1942, ready for issue.

Mack EHUT   Truck, 5-ton, 4x2, Tractor   1942

GENERAL

Fourth and last in the mixed batch of 900 Mack EH-series
Defense Aid trucks in 1942 were 180 cab-over tractors
with semi-trailers. The total number of semi-trailers
(Mack ST20, see following entry) was 320, supplied with
EHT (qv) and the subject EHUT tractor trucks. The
chassis Nos. for the EHUTs were EHUT1D1224-1303 and
1304-1403, the last group with a different gearbox. USA
registration Nos. were W-526296-375 and 526056-155 but
all were destined for Lend-Lease shipments. The QMC
Contract No. was 12933, as for the others (see preceding
entries). At least some of the EHUT/ST20 combinations
went to Britain, others were possibly shipped to British
or Commonwealth recipients at alternative overseas
destinations. It is believed that the 900 Defense Aid Mack
EH/EHU/EHT/EHUT trucks with their varying
specifications were assembled from stockpiled
components at the factory, clearing the way for
concentration on production of strictly military (semi-)
tactical models.

PHYSICAL

Except for the cab-over-engine configuration and thus a
shorter wheelbase and slightly less overall length the
EHUT was similar to the EHT.

TECHNICAL

The standard commercial EHUT had the Mack EN310
engine but the EN354 was optional (as was the Buda
6DT389 diesel) and these militarized EHUTs had the
EN354, which turned out 112 bhp. The first 80 had the
TR31 5-speed direct top gearbox, the others also had the
TR31 but with different (optional) gear ratios and
overdrive top. All had air-brakes, with trailer
connections. Tyres were 9.00-20, on tractor and trailer.

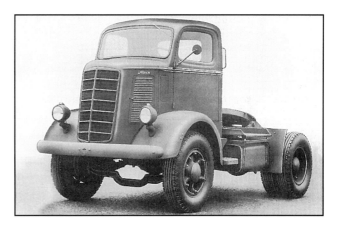

Top: EHUT complete with ST20 semi-trailer, ex-works in July
1942.

Above and *below:* Three-quarter front and rear views of the
tractor unit.

Mack ST20   Semi-Trailer, 8-ton, 2-wheel   1942

Along with the 320 EHT and EHUT tractor trucks which Mack delivered during 1942 for Defense Aid through the US Government, the company supplied 320 matching Model ST20 semi-trailers, also covered by QMC Contract 12933.

The trailer couplings and associated parts were also made and installed by Mack. USA registration Nos. were 0140873-1192. The trailers were classed at a gross-weight rating of eight tons. The cast spoke wheels and 9.00-20 tyres

corresponded with those of the tractive units. The pictures reproduced here show the chassis built-up and knocked-down in twin-unit pack for shipment overseas. The body (shown on preceding pages) measured 216 x 90 in.

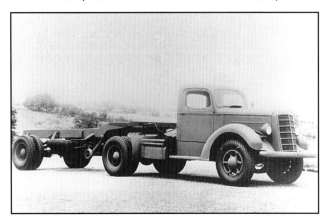

Mack EH   Truck, 5-ton, 4x2, Cargo   1943

GENERAL

In 1942 Mack initiated the development of a military pattern semi-tactical variant of the EH 5-tonner for the QMC (Contract W-2425-QM-230) for Defense Aid distribution. The new truck was ready for quantity production in 1943 and the Ordnance Department placed an initial order for 2,450 cargo trucks (W-670-ORD-3191) of which 2,350 were delivered in 1943, the remainder in early 1944. A follow-up order (Contract W-670-ORD-4783) was for a further 1,000 in 1944. They were known also as 5-6-ton trucks. There were also orders for bus and tractor-truck chassis (*qv*). The cargo truck chassis s/n were EH1D3976-6426 for the first and 6901-7900 for the second batch. The USA registrations were 4410531-2980 and 546820-7819 respectively. From the total of 3,450, 2,400 were supplied to Britain (S/M 2429) where they were known as 3-, 5- or 6-ton GS load carriers. British WD Nos. included L5217013-517 and 5581302-2162. Unit value in 1944 was $3,741.

PHYSICAL

Sturdy austere front end with flat-top mudguards, radiator guard, open cab with half-doors and folding canvas top and side curtains, 12-ft wooden body (by Perfection Body Co.), all finished in lustreless olive drab. Wheelbase 170 in. Overall dimensions 271 x 96 x 113 (reducable to 94) in. Weight 10,500 lb, gross 20,500 lb.

TECHNICAL

Own 110-bhp EN354 6-cyl. L-head petrol engine with TR31 direct-top 5-speed gearbox. Dual-reduction rear axle. Air-actuated brakes. 20x8 Budd disc wheels with 9.00-20 tyres. 6-Volt electrical equipment.

Top and *above:* USA 4411341 factory-fresh, with troop seats swung up.

Below: Prepared in the UK for British Army service. (Note the 'off-side' direction indicator, bridge plate, etc.).

Mack EHT   Truck, 5-ton, 4x2, Tractor   1943

GENERAL

In addition to the military-pattern EH Cargo truck of 1943-44 there were two limited-production derivatives: the short-wheelbase (146-in.) tractor with fifth-wheel coupling for semi-trailers, shown here, and a long-wheelbase (230-in.) bus chassis, the latter with a dash-to-end-of-frame length of 310 in. Both were part of the initial order (Contract W-670-ORD-3191 of March 16, 1943). Of the tractor only 50 were built, with chassis s/n EHT1D 2432-481. They were supplied with USA registrations 4413081-130, all delivered in 1943. Book value in 1944 was listed as $3,505 each. Some were used by the Royal Navy in Australia.

PHYSICAL

Same front end and soft-top cab as Cargo version but shorter frame, with semi-trailer turntable. Both had circular 41-gal. (Imp.) fuel tank for radius of action up to 350 miles (empty). Radiator surround, bonnet/hood top and cowl were characteristic of EH series. Wheelbase 146 in. Overall dimensions 219 x 92 x 87 in. Weight 8,800 lb, gross 20,800 lb.

TECHNICAL

Own EN354 L-head Six engine with 3.875 x 5.0 in. bore and stroke, cubic capacity 354 cu.in. (5.8 litres), with 5.5:1 compression ratio. 110 bhp at governed 2,620 rpm. Zenith updraft carburettor. Own TR31 direct-top 5-speed gearbox and RA44 dual-reduction rear axle with ratio 8.59:1 (providing top speed of 35.2 mph at governed engine speed). Bendix-Westinghouse air brakes. Tyres 9.00-20. 6-Volt electrics.

All three photographs show second tractor truck built: USA 4413082, in June 1943. Single headlamp suggests British or Commonwealth destination.

Mack EH Miscellany

In addition to the EH-series trucks presented in the foregoing pages there were several more related models which are worthy of mention, including some which resembled the EH but were not, i.e. the elusive ND and NH of 1940-41, all of which had EH-series cab and sheet metal. Of the ND only one (s/n ND1D1001) was supplied to the US Engineers in Albany, New York, on October 5, 1940. It was a dump truck with EN310 engine.

Of the NH the first two (s/n NH1D1001D and 2D) were dump trucks with Buda 6DT389 diesel engine. They were shipped on November 12, 1940, to the Naval Powder Factory at Indianhead in Maryland. The third and fourth were NH1D1003D and 4D, both shipped on

March 4, 1941 for the US Navy, also to Indianhead. Of this pair the first was a long-wheelbase chassis with Cummins AA600 diesel engine and a stake rack body, the other a tractor unit with the same engine.

The 100 230-in. wheelbase chassis on Contract W-670-ORD-3191 of March 16, 1943, which covered mainly military pattern EH trucks (qv), are an intangible lot. The chassis were numbered EH1D6426-6525 and the USA registration numbers were 4412981-3080. Superior Coach was contracted (33-019-2210) for 100 37-passenger schoolbus-type bodies and the vehicles were renumbered USA 20741076-175. They were allocated to the British (S/M 6113 of August 21, 1944) and destined for New Zealand.

Reportedly the Kiwis transformed quite a few EHs to right-hand drive forward-control buses. By September 1945 the New Zealand Railways and Road Services operated a fleet of 248 Macks, probably including the 100 subject chassis. The military pattern EH front end on a bus chassis now survives only on drawings.

Quartermaster Corps and Ordnance 1940-45 prime contracts indicate a total of 4,564 EH-series Macks. Added to these should be the handful of USN and USMC jobs and direct cash-and-carry sales to foreign military customers, i.e. prior to the enactment of the Lend-Lease agreement in early 1941. Many of these Macks continued in civil service until well into the 1960s

Mack 75　　　Fire Truck, Class 750　　　1942

GENERAL

A well-known fire-fighter of the WWII period was the Truck, Fire, Powered, Pumper, Class 750, 4x2, 750-gpm, to give it its full name. In the US Army, fire trucks were not a QMC or Ordnance responsibility; they were issued by the Corps of Engineers. Chassis used and suppliers of equipment were many and the type featured here (the largest pumper supplied by the Corps of Engineers) could have equipment furnished by American LaFrance-Foamite or one of four other specialist manufacturers. These appliances were used for fighting structural fires in Army posts, camps, stations. The subject rig used EH cab and front-end sheet metal and was built expressly for military and civilian fire service, featuring a special engine with 7-bearing crankshaft and other refinements to better cope with extended periods of stationary operation. The USA registrations included 502063-99 for a group of 37 supplied under Contract 13004 in 1942.

PHYSICAL

Conventional 2½-5-ton-type 170-in.-wheelbase chassis/cab with midship-mounted fire pump, booster water tank (150 gal.), hose body and fire-fighting equipment. Overall dimensions 273 x 93 x 88 in. Weight 12,020 lb, gross 16,250 lb. Crew six.

TECHNICAL

Own ENF510A Thermodyne 6-cyl. overhead-valve engine developing 155-160 bhp at 2,600 rpm. 5-speed direct-top gearbox. 6.86 rear axle. Semi-hydraulic brakes. 9.00-20 tyres. 12-Volt electrics. Hale ZD engine-driven centrifugal pump with capacity of 250 gpm at 250 psi up to 750 gpm at 120 psi.

Top and *above:* Standard military pumper on 2½-ton 4x2 Mack 75 chassis/cab with own bodywork and equipment.

Below: Variant with entirely open bodywork

Mack Fire Trucks

During the 1930s Mack became one of the world's premier fire truck producers and the various branches of the armed services became regular customers for more or less militarised models. From 1940 until 1944 Mack delivered 97 units for Ordnance and 757 for other agencies with a total dollar value of 4.18 million. Shown here are some typical examples on own 4x2 chassis.

Top: Type 25 Class 125 with Hardie HP piston pump on E-series 1½-ton chassis (USA 502471), 1942, and a Class 500 Pumper (USA 50601)on 2½-ton EE model chassis equipped with open cab and all the civvy-style chrome-plated brightwork.

Above: Crash truck of the US Navy on EHU chassis, 1940, and EH-style ladder truck, the latter supplied to the USAAF's Wright Field near Dayton, Ohio. The Air Force also had at least 200 of the Type 25 crash trucks, known chassis serials being 25S1010 to 1209

Below: Mack 75 Class 750 production lines in the Allentown plant.

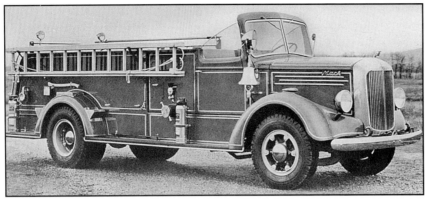

In 1940-41 Mack supplied many pumpers like the one on the left, one of seven produced for the US Navy Yard at Charleston, North Carolina.

Below: This Model 95LS 1000-gpm pumper with doorless bodywork was also for the US Navy; it was delivered in February 1942. The 95 had a 707-cid engine, developing 200 bhp at 2,500 rpm.

Bottom: In February 1943 the 19LS crash truck made its appearance. It had a 1,000-gal. tank and could pump 250 gpm of fog at 600 psi through its two foam nozzles.

Mack FPD   Truck, 6-ton, 4x2, Dump   1940

GENERAL

During 1940-42 Mack built 365 of these FP-series hybrid chassis: modern EH-style cab and front end on a classic chain-drive chassis. Included was a batch of 40 ordered by the military in 1940, equipped with 5-yd dump body, under Contract 8496. They were powered by the optional Buda diesel engine and therefore designated FPD. The 40 dump trucks were all delivered in the same year and numbered USA W51023-062. The purchase price was $5,060 each. (Book value in 1944 was stated as $5,413.) In some publications the subject vehicles were referred to as 5-tonners. The FP's standard engine was the 100-bhp EN354 petrol/gasoline L-head Six, a larger-bore version of the contemporary EN310; the diesel engine in the FPD was an extra-cost ($1,550) factory-installed option.

PHYSICAL

The FP(D) looked like an EH variant but was easily distinguishable by its exposed drive chains. It had a 158-in. wheelbase and rode on 9.75-20 tyres. Overall dimensions of the chassis/cab were about 235 x 90 x 86 in. The FPD in dump truck form weighed 13,750 lb.

TECHNICAL

Buda-Lanova 6DT468 6-cyl. diesel engine of 468 cu.in. piston displacement (bore and stroke 4.25 x 5.5 in.). Power output 100 bhp at 2,000 rpm. Max. torque 300 lb.-ft at 1,200 rpm. 5-speed gearbox. Banjo-type jackshaft with chain drive. Rear wheel hubs mounted on 'dead' axle beam.

Top: FPD had Mack Diesel name plate on sides.

Above: Typical FP(D) dump truck.

Below: Rear chassis view showing chain drive.

Mack FG Truck, 10-ton, 4x2, Dump 1942

GENERAL

The Series F 4x2 Super Duty Mack chassis of the late 1930s and early '40s were used mostly for medium-capacity construction trucks like dump and concrete mixer units. Designated FG, FH, FJ, FK, FN, etc., they were essentially similar, the differences being mainly in tyre sizes and chassis component reinforcements to cope with increasing gross weights, from 35,000 to 50,000 lb. Petrol engines were standard but most could be ordered with diesel power. In 1942 a batch of 25 FGs with Hoist Dump bodies was acquired by the QMC under Contract 13275/ORD-670-3347, on behalf of the British Government (S/M 2374) and shipped PKD to Australia, where GM-H reassembled them. Their USA registrations were 57972-996. (In early 1943 the British ordered a further 25 on FT chassis, Contract S/M 2813, WD Nos. L4688588-612; the first 12 at least were assembled by Bristol Tramways in February.) US Army Engineers had a number of FJs with 10-yd dump bodies.

PHYSICAL

Even by the standards of 1942 this was an old-fashioned looking machine with classic but proven features like chain drive and a hard-top C-cab with tiny doors and roll-up curtains instead of side windows. Body was raised by hydraulic ram with T-bar pushing rearwards against a pair of curved wedges, forcing the body up, with a hefty chain acting as a stop.

TECHNICAL

Engine (standard) was Mack 6-cyl. L-head CF468 (468 cu.in., 4.25 x 5.5 in.) petrol unit, developing 117 bhp at 2,400 rpm and 317 lb.-ft of torque at 1,000 rpm. Compression ratio 5.0:1. Chain-drive from jackshaft sprockets to rear wheels.

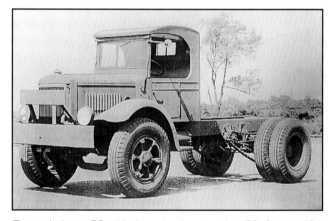

Top and *above:* FG with dump body raised (s/n FG1C1152; USA 57980) and as chassis/cab (USA 57985).
Below: Survivor in Australia (s/n FG1C1162). It has now been beautifully restored, albeit in mufti.

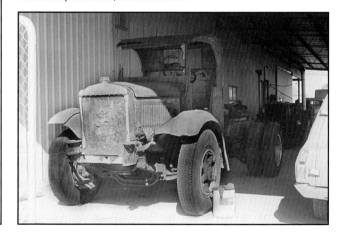

Mack LFT   Truck, 12-ton, 4x2, Tractor   1942

GENERAL

The L-series heavy-duty models were launched in 1940 and produced in large numbers throughout the decade, except during 1942-44 when civilian truck production was 'suspended for the duration'. Among the last built in 1942 were five LFT tractor trucks for the US Army. Supplied under Contract W-670-ORD-3504 (Production Order T5125) they were allocated War Department numbers 534940-944. The vehicles sported the same front end and cab styling as the contemporary NR, except for the austere finish of the latter. In addition to the Army, the US Navy procured an unspecified quantity for hauling helium (for blimps) on specially adapted semi-trailers

PHYSICAL

Heavy-duty tractive unit of typical new 1940s' Mack appearance: sturdy and only slightly 'rounded'. Compared with post-war production these early models had the radiator filler cap under the bonnet/hood rather than exposed. The LFT's standard wheelbase size was 140 in., for an overall length of 218 in. Height was just under 95 in. Weight (typical model) 11,300 lb.

TECHNICAL

Standard engine was the EN431 L-head Six of 124 bhp (with 133-bhp EN471 and 107-bhp END405 diesel also available). Gearbox was 5-speed TR32 with direct or overdrive top, or the Duplex (dual-range) TAD-32. Rear axle had dual reduction. For the commercial range there was choice of many options. Tyres 9.00-20 or 10.00-20; 22-in. rims were offered also. Westinghouse air brakes. 12-Volt electrics.

Top: US Navy rig for transportation of helium.

Above: Civilian tractor with military-style brush guard.

Below: Dimensional sketch for varying wheelbase sizes.

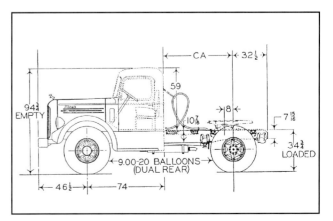

Cab-overs or Traffic Types

Top: Half a dozen Mack LJU trucks with tank bodies for the US Navy, July 1942. The LJU was in production during the 1940s and into the '50s and unlike the EHU (qv) had full forward control with the engine between the seats. Standard spec was 135-in. wheelbase, 135-bhp EN471 L-head Six with TR32 gearbox, RA62 dual-reduction axle, vacuum-assisted hydraulic brakes, 10.00-20 tyres.

Left: In 1948 the US Navy procured this 7-ton LMU. It was similar to the LJU but heavier, with EP 163-bhp 611-cid Thermodyne overhead-valve engine, TRD37 Duplex (5F1Rx2) transmission, RA59 rear axle, air brakes and 11.00-22 tyres. The cab of the NJU 4x4 (qv) was a militarised (and taller) version of that of the LJU and LMU models.

Below: Another commercial COE (Traffic Type in Mack parlance) was this CJ 6x4 of around 1940. It worked at the US Navy Yard in Portsmouth, NH, where it hauled 40-ton sections of submarines from production site to final assembly area.

Mack NJU-1, -2   Truck, 5-6-ton, 4x4, Tractor   1941

GENERAL

Four-wheel drive Macks have never been common but on December 9, 1940, the company was contracted (W-398-QM-8977) for 700 4x4 tractor trucks for the US Army, intended mainly for ponton-carrying semi-trailers. Designated NJU they derived from the commercial 'Traffic Type', militarised and redesigned to have 4WD. Delivery took place in 1941 (694) and early 1942 (6). 692 were Ponton tractors, Model NJU-1, the remaining eight being NJU-2, for Topographical semi-trailers. Price was around $6,000 each. Chassis s/n, NJU-1: NJU9D1001-1548 and 1557-1700; NJU-2: NJU9D1549-56. USA Nos., NJU-1: 51761, 51763-52420 and 52457-89; NJU-2: 52490-97. From as early as November 1941 a portion of the NJU-1s was released to the British in Egypt and renumbered, e.g. H1324948-5067. The US Army standardised the Autocar-built equivalent.

PHYSICAL

Tall COE 4x4 tractor with coupling for semi-trailer. Wheelbase 148 in. Overall dimensions 237 x 96 x 114 in. Weight 16,580 lb (NJU-1). NJU-2 did not have the steel box behind the cab and weighed 16,230 lb.

TECHNICAL

Own EN532 6-cyl. L-head (side-valve) engine developing 136 bhp at 2,400 rpm. TR320D 5-speed gearbox. Timken T76 2-speed transfer case. Timken double-reduction axles, at front with Rzeppa CV joints. Air-actuated brakes. Gar Wood 3U615 winch below bumper. Disc wheels with 12.00-20 tyres (9.75-20 before s/n 1066).

Top: Early model, USA 51826, with 9.75-20 tyres and full rear mudguards.

Above: Pilot model, USA 51761 (note detail differences).

Below: Late production unit on 12.00-20 tyres.

Top: Early (upper right) and late (left) models, with USA Nos. 51826 and 51828 respectively. The former had s/n 1065 and was photographed in April 1941. The third was in post-war French Army service and sports locally-made rear mudguards.

Middle: NJU-1 coupled to 25-ton Ponton (pontoon) dropframe semi-trailer, Model 1940, in service with Corps of Engineers. Notice the mix of late-production features and the early USA number, suggesting upgrading. The trailer measured 375 x 97 in. and weighed 7,500 lb. These pontoon and bridging equipment trailers were built by Dart Truck Co., Electric Wheel Co., Fruehauf Trailer Co. and Trailer Company of America.

Bottom: Single loads (and dolly in tow) during stateside exercises in 1941.

Mack NB-1   Truck, 2½-ton, 6x4, Searchlight   1940

GENERAL

In late 1939 the US Government ordered a large number of searchlight trucks, including 368 from Mack. The Contract for the Macks was W-398-QM-7517, dated December 20, 1939, and the chassis s/n were NB4S1001-1368. Delivery took place in 1940, with US Army registrations W601455-1822. The SNL Group was G629, the Vehicle Code 6040-540. Technical Manuals were TM10-1188 (PL) and -1189 (MM). The chassis/cab cost $ 2,050. The steel body was equipped for searchlight work, with ramps, clamps, brackets, etc. but could be used also for hauling general cargo. Although officially referred to as Model NB-1, there never actually was a Mack NB-2. The other contractors for searchlight trucks were Federal and GMC but only the Macks had a 4-door cab.

PHYSICAL

The NB was a militarised commercial EEU-derived COE semi-forward-control truck with an extended 5-seat cab to accommodate the searchlight crew. The cab had four doors, identical (per side) front and rear. The steel body had tall bows to clear the Sperry searchlight equipment, with a tarpaulin to suit. Overall dimensions were 288 x 96 x 139 in., wheelbase 172 (BC 44) in. Weight 10,630 lb, GVW rating 15,630 lb.

TECHNICAL

Mack FO (Continental M6253) 6-cyl. L-head engine, 253 cid (3.5 x 4.375 in.), 78 bhp. Warner 4-speed gearbox with Timken 2-speed (direct and 1.87:1) auxiliary. Timken rear axles, ratio 6.6:1. Hydraulic brakes (Lockheed) with Hydrovac. Cast spoke wheels with 7.00-20 tyres, dual rear. 6-Volt electrics.

Top and above: Side and three-quarter front views with canvas in place.

Below: Canvas rolled up.

Mack LMSW-23   Truck, 5-ton, 6x4, Wrecker   1941

GENERAL

In 1941 the British Purchasing Commission (BPC), with its office on 15 Broad Street in New York City, placed a first order for Mack 6x4 chassis with recovery equipment to supplement the British Army's Scammell SV/2S Heavy Breakdown Tractors (which, presumably, were not being delivered fast enough to meet demands). The US QMC contracted Mack for an initial 193 LMSW chassis/cabs (W-398-QM-9756; chassis s/n LM2D1028-1220) and supplied these to Britain (S/M 2047) with Gar Wood BC wrecker unit. The WD Nos. allocated were H777053-092 (40, for RASC) and H4655373-525 (153, for RAOC).

PHYSICAL

Militarized commercial LM Six-Wheeler (LMSW-23) chassis/cab with oversize tyres, radiator guard, drawbar gear front and rear, front end counterweights and other special features. Gar Wood steel body, sliding jib and equipment. Wheelbase 166 (BC 55) in. Overall dimensions 285 x 98 x 117 in. Weight 23,760 lb.

TECHNICAL

Own EP 6-cyl. 160-bhp 611-cid overhead-valve petrol engine, driving SW318 tandem rear axle bogie via TRD15 Duplex (5F1Rx2) transmission and power divider between the rear differentials. Axle ratio 9.02:1. Westinghouse air brakes. 12-Volt electrics. Steel spoked wheels with 13.50-20 tyres. Gar Wood 401 main and crane winches, chain-driven. Hand-operated boom. Hoisting capacity 10,000 lb (3 ft from end of chassis).

Top: Newly delivered to the RASC in Britain

Above: Jib extended. Notice the winches mounted amidships.

Below: Spare wheel was installed on reassembly in UK.

Mack LMSW-39   Truck, 5-ton, 6x4, Wrecker   1942

GENERAL

The second batch of LMSW recovery vehicles with
sliding jib comprised 181 units, ordered under Contract
DA-W670-QM-77 (later ORD-W-670-3185) and supplied to
the British under S/M 2109. The chassis s/n ran from
LM2D1236 to 1416. These vehicles were destined for the
Far East and shipped directly to India where WD Nos.
were allocated locally (they included H6287726-730). End
users were the RASC (86) and RAOC (95). The
specification differed but slightly from the LMSW-23 and
the Gar Wood-design wrecker unit was now
manufactured by Mack, with power winches from Heil.
Like before, the chassis/cabs were delivered in PKD form,
chassis in one case, cabs in another, with the wrecker
unit separately.

PHYSICAL

The LMSW-39 resembled the preceding LMSW-23 (qv)
but there were detail differences in the Mack-built
wrecker unit and most if not all were supplied with a
heat shield atop the cab. At the factory both types were
painted British Khaki No. 3. Dimensions were similar to
the LMSW-23.

TECHNICAL

Detail changes when compared with the LMSW-23
included a 6- (vs 4-) bladed engine fan, sealed-beam
headlamps and a TRDX-15 transmission with a different
low ratio in the auxiliary gears. Ex-factory the tyre size
was 14.00-20. Interestingly, the tail and convoy lamps
were CMP, supplied by Ford Canada and GM Canada for
the LMSW-23 and -39 respectively.

Top: LMSW-39 had Heil winches and a Mack-built body and
crane.

Above: Side view showing winches mounted one above the
other.

Below: This model had the spare wheel carrier as original
equipment.

Mack LMSW-53   Truck, 5-ton, 6x4, Wrecker   1942

GENERAL

Mack's third order for LMSW chassis/cabs for recovery
vehicles came from Canada. In the US Government
supply system it was covered by Contract
USP-8673-CAN-183, for which the Canadians issued
three acquisition orders: CDLV-331, -406 and -490,
followed by -587. The total quantity was 130 vehicles and
their chassis s/n were LM2D1470-1599. They differed
from the British-specification wreckers mainly in having
a different superstructure, from Gar Wood in Detroit,
with double swinging booms. This equipment was
installed in Canada by Chrysler Corp. in Windsor,
Ontario. Like the British, the Canadians officially called
them Tractors, Breakdown, Heavy.

PHYSICAL

Like the preceding LMSW models -23 and -39, the -53
was basically a commercial truck, brought up to military
specifications by installing larger tyres - single rear - with
flat-section front mudguards, spring-mounted pintle
hooks front and rear, etc. The crane was of the
twin-boom type with side brace legs and a tubular
superstructure for a tarpaulin (to disguise its special
purpose). Overall dimensions 294-325 x 99 x 118-129 in.
Operational weight 30,000 lb.

TECHNICAL

The chassis specification was essentially the same as on
earlier types but with changes to the brake system which
now incorporated a trailer brakes hand control mounted
on the steering column. The crane (Gar Wood CA8P)
could lift eight tons on a single boom, 16 on both (using
two part lines). The power winch (Gar Wood 5M) had a
capacity of 40,000 lb.

Top: Newly-fitted Gar Wood wrecking equipment (by Chrysler).

Above: Chassis/cab as supplied by Mack.

Below: One of about two dozen of the Netherlands Army, circa
1952.

Mack LMSW-57   Truck, 5-ton, 6x4, Wrecker   1943/44

GENERAL

Last of the LMSW-based wrecker/recovery trucks was the open-cab LMSW-57, again supplied to Canada, where the Vehicle Code was 200646-C-BRKD-2. Canadian contracts were CDLV-1516 and -1659. The chassis s/n ran from LM2D1617 to 1776, indicating a total of 160. Deliveries took place in 1944. After WWII had ended, the Canadians left many of their vehicles in Europe and surplus wreckers entered service with several NATO forces, others being released for civilian use. Some were reconditioned (5th Echelon rebuild) and provided with new enclosed cabs, recognisable by the door vent windows.

PHYSICAL

The LMSW-57 was the same as the -53 model but had a soft-top folding cab like the late-production Mack NM and NR (qv). It was of steel construction with folding windscreen and canvas top with side curtains and a roll-up rear flap. The body (Code 6G2) was 92 in. long and had three stowage lockers on either side. Equipment included oxy-acetylene welding and cutting outfit. Wooden ground rollers were carried in brackets on the crane booms.

TECHNICAL

Like the other LMSW wreckers this model had the Mack EP Thermodyne 160-bhp 611-cid engine. The cooling fan had six blades, like the LMSW-39 (-23 and -53 had four). The Canadians specified 14.00-20 tyres. The track width was 83 in. front, 75.25 rear.

Top: Surplussed vehicle in Holland. This example carries telescopic booms, a later modification.

Above: Chassis/cab as delivered by Mack in October 1943.

Below: Post-war rebuilt unit with new cab, early 1950s.

LMSW Miscellany

Top: Mack LMSW-series recovery vehicles were variously known as 4-5-, 5- and 6-ton Wreckers or Breakdown tractors. Shown is the very first, in 1941, as chassis/cab and built-up with body, winches and crane.

Left: The British and Commonwealth forces frequently used these Macks for tank hauling, like here in North Africa. Postwar users included the armies of Belgium, the Netherlands, Portugal and South Africa.

Below left: Canadian Army twin-boom types in action. They have WD Nos. (CH)4244715 and 4244764 respectively.

Below: Bird's eye view of an LMSW-57 showing position of crane booms and superstructure prior to installing tarpaulin and metamorphosing the wrecker as a 'covered wagon', i.e. a more common GS cargo truck.

Mack EXBX   Truck, 18-ton, 6x4, Tank Transporter   1940

GENERAL

In 1940 Mack shipped 260 large-capacity fuel tank trucks to Europe. Most had originally been ordered for the French Army but the outbreak of war caused the shipments to be diverted to Britain. The first lot of 110 (s/n EXBX2D1001-1110) was covered by French Contract F134, British S/M 2038 and 2049. A further 100 (s/n 1111-1210) came from Contract F45 (British S/M 2014). They arrived as 4,800-gallon (US) refuelling trucks, c/w pump, meter, hose reel and nozzle, but the British had a more urgent need for tank carriers and had most of them converted to flat-platform trucks capable of carrying tanks of up to 18 tons. New WD Nos. were intermingled with those of similar trucks built by White but within ranges 769901-770098, 4471890-909 and 4588129-132. An unspecified number were used as bulk fuel carriers in North Africa.

PHYSICAL

A somewhat dated looking American truck with rather small cab in relation to its imposing overall appearance. Early tank carrier conversions had folding 'Bees Knees' ramps, later all were fitted with a built-up type. Wheelbase 209 in. Overall 370 x 121 x 136 in. (ramps folded); with the new ramps 353 x 121 x 99 (cab) in. Weight 26,880 and 22,110 lb resp.

TECHNICAL

Own EO Thermodyne 519-cid OHV petrol 6-cyl. engine, developing max. 145 bhp at 2,350 rpm, with 5-speed direct-top gearbox. Tandem bogie with double-reduction Mack axles and power divider. Ratio 8.17 or (from s/n 1126) 9.02:1. Tyres 10.50-24, dual rear. Air-actuated brakes.

Top: Anglicized L770015 ready for delivery to RASC.

Above: Later model with non-folding removable ramps.

Below: As bulk fuel tanker in the Western Desert.

Mack EXBX-2 Truck, 18-ton, 6x4, Tank Transporter 1940/41

GENERAL

Following the earlier batches totalling 210 ex-French Contract Mack EXBX trucks, there was a further and last lot of 50 which differed in having a Timken-Detroit tandem bogie and minor other differences. The British S/M (Supply Mechanical) order No. was 2014 (which also covered a hundred of the earlier vehicles). The chassis serials were EXBX4D1001-1050. Of all these 50 + 100 trucks when received 75 carried a tank and ancillaries by Columbian Steel Equipment and the other 75 by Heil Co. The tanks were all-steel 8-compartment with a capacity of 4,800 US gallons. Following British service as tank transporters some of the trucks were rebodied yet again, now as GS load carriers.

PHYSICAL

Externally the EXBX-2 looked similar to the preceding EXBX (qv). Main points of recognition were the rear springs, near-flat rear axle half shaft flanges and 22-in. tyres.

TECHNICAL

Engine and transmission same as EXBX2D1111-1210, but different rear axles and suspension, all supplied by Timken-Detroit (Model SD353WX1 axles with overhead double-reduction, ratio overall 7.33:1). Inverted semi-elliptic leaf springs had their ends resting on top of the axle housings, rather than below them as on the Mack bogie. Wheels with 22x9-10-in. rims and 10.50-22 tyres. Air brakes.

Top: Newly camouflaged with steel body and early-type loading ramps.

Above: White blot on bonnet (hood) in front of driver was gas-detection paint.

Below: EXBX-2 in original refueller form was finished in Mack Brewster green No. 815, with chromium-plated bumper.

Six-wheelers Miscellany

Left: The FK Series was current from 1938 to '41. This is a Cummins-powered FKSW of late 1939 with low-boy semi-trailer serving the US Navy and seen here with a battleship's gun turret.

Below: On the left is a 1940 FKSW-based mobile field dynamometer of Aberdeen Proving Ground. Known as M5 it carried two 750-gpm Hale pumps for a retarding power of 20,000 lb. It measured drawbar pull capacity of tanks and other military vehicles. On the right is addition M6 of 1941, using a Mack LPSW chassis with 195-bhp EY engine.

Bottom: The 1944 Mack-built Power Absorption Trailer (PAT) when coupled to the M5 or M6 added 15,000 lb of retardation capacity via a heavy-duty Mack truck bogie. They had an unmistakable Mack family likeness.

Mack NR-1   Truck, 10-ton, 6x4, Cargo   1940

GENERAL

First of the ubiquitous NR-series Mack diesel military six-wheelers was the NR-1 which succeeded the EXBX in 1940 and was of broadly similar general appearance. The British procured 90 - on cash-and-carry terms - for use in the Middle and Near East. They carried s/n NR4D1001D-1090D. The contract numbers were A-403 (BPC) and S/M code TT2/1. The trucks were shipped in chassis/cab form, partly knocked down (PKD) in single-unit packs. The wooden bodies were procured separately and fitted at the point of destination. WD numbers were taken from the range 1263030-8529, a block allotted to the Middle East for vehicles shipped there directly from non-UK sources.

PHYSICAL

Outwardly the NR-1 was much like the Mack heavy-duty trucks of the 1930s, with its square contours, vertical windscreen and radiator. Unlike the EXBX (*qv*) the NR had a hefty brushguard protecting headlamps and radiator, and single rear tyres. The heat shield on the cab roof was standard. Overall dimensions (chassis/cab) 326 x 94 x 103 in. approx. Wheelbase 201 (BC 55) in. Weight, chassis/cab 18,400 lb plus about 4,000 lb for the body.

TECHNICAL

Mack-Lanova ED diesel engine, 6-cyl., 519-cid, developing 131 bhp at 2,000 rpm. Two interchangeable cylinder heads. TR12 Duplex OD-top gearbox (with 'fast' and 'slow' ratios in all gears). SW30S tandem bogie with power divider and double-reduction 9.02:1 axles. Dayton 6-spoke wheels with 10.50-24 front and 13.50-20 rear tyres. Air brakes. Four batteries for 24-V starting, 12-V lighting.

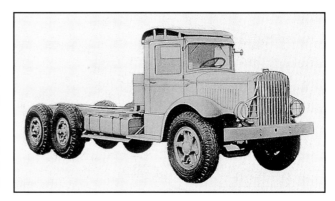

Top: Ready for issue to RASC in Egypt: s/n NR4D1066D, August 1940.

Above: Chassis/cab as shipped by Mack.

Below: L1266046 carrying gun in Egypt. Note the winch.

Mack NR-2 and -3   Truck, 10-ton, 6x4, Cargo   1941

GENERAL

The Mack NR-2 was the first of the NRs to have the
contemporary L-series styling for front end and cab
(Model 270), albeit militarized. The BPC in New York
ordered 330 under S/M 2036 for shipment direct to the
Middle East, in 1941. Chassis s/n were NR4D1091D-
1420D. A further 61, designated NR-3, came under Lend-
Lease (NR4D1421D-1481D), Contract DA-W-398-QM-20,
dated June 16, 1941; S/M 2075. These trucks were
shipped in PKD form and their bodies came, separately,
from Kramer Body and Equipment Co. It was a 15x8-ft
wooden GS type with 20-in. sides and a duck tarpaulin.
WD Nos. were within the range 1303831-1312330. Mainly
used by the RASC for long-distance haulage they were
variously referred to as 10-ton and 11-ton GS Load
Carriers. The NR-1 and -2 cost the British an average
$8,483.86.

PHYSICAL

Militarized heavy six-wheeler with large single tyres all
round, brushguard and heat shield. Overall dimensions
322 x 103 x 100 (cab) in. Wheelbase 201 in. to centre of
bogie; distance between rear axles 55 in. Weight 20,415
lb. All had 6-gal. (Imp.) Thermos water tank on right of
scuttle.

TECHNICAL

Mack-Lanova ED 6-cyl. diesel with 10-speed Duplex
transmission: TRDS17 direct-top on s/n 1091-1188,
TRD12 overdrive-top on 1189-1420 and TRD37 overdrive-
top on 1421-1481. Rear axle ratio 7.32 on s/n 1091-1188,
9.02:1 on all others. Tyre size 10.50-24 front and 13.50-20
rear on NR-2, 11.00-24 front and 14.00-20 rear on NR-3.

Top: NR-2 prior to knock-down for shipment.

Above: NR-3 had slightly different body compared with NR-2.

Below: NR-3 carrying field gun, Jan. 1942. Note ramp on side.

Mack NR-4   Truck, 10-ton, 6x4, Transporter   1941

GENERAL

On August 21, 1941, the US QMC placed an order (DA-W-398-QM-57) for 200 NR-series chassis/cabs specifically for use as light tank carriers by the British Army which received them (along with 189 NR-5 cargo trucks) in 1941-42. The chassis s/n were given as NR4D1482D-1592D and 1643D-1731D but also as 1482D-1681D, both totalling 200 (see also NR-5). The British contract number for the NR4 was S/M2279. The carriers were used primarily for the US light tanks (Stuart) and often referred to as 13-tonners. Like the NR-2, -3 and -5 the NR-4 had a heat shield over the cab and a 6-gal. Thermos water tank furnished by American Coach & Body Co. The US War Department valued the NR-4 at $8,846.

PHYSICAL

The NR-4 resembled the NR-2, -3 and -5 but had a different open type light tank transporter body with special equipment like loading ramps, ramp guides, chock blocks and a 12-ton hydraulic jack to support rear of chassis when loading and unloading. Body was also six inches longer. Weight was 24,700 lb, laden with M3 light tank the GVW approached 50,000 lb. NR-4 and -5 were delivered in Coronado tan, dull finish.

TECHNICAL

Essentially as NR-3 but 18- vs 16-ply rear tyres (14.00-20) and heavier springs but with fewer leaves (front 8 vs 11, rear 15 vs 17). The tank carrying platform was made by Perfection Steel Body Co. and measured 184 x 102 in.

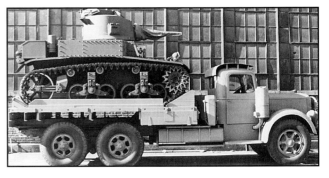

Top: Factory-fresh, probably the prototype.

Above and *below:* Loaded with a Stuart light tank (early-1941 M3 with welded/cast homogenous rounded turret and riveted hull) in Dec. 1941.

Mack NR-5   Truck, 10-ton, 6x4, Cargo   1941

GENERAL

The NR-5 was a GS load carrier again and covered by
the same US contract as the NR-4, i.e. DA-W-398-QM-57.
The British contract was S/M 2075. The chassis s/n were
listed as NR4D1682D-1870D, totalling 189 units. One
source gives different numbers, viz. NR4D1593D-1642D
and 1732D-1870D, also adding up to 189. If anything, this
shows that NR-4 and -5 chassis were built as one group.
They had been ordered by the British Purchasing
Commission at the same time and delivery was also
combined: 138 in 1941 and 251 in early 1942. At least 50
went to the UK (L4857912-961). The completed NR-5,
bodied as cargo truck, was valued at $8,910 in the WD
listing.

PHYSICAL

Similar to the NR-4 except that it had a wooden cargo
body like the NR-2, with top bows, ridge poles and
canvas cover. Overall dimensions were 322 x 103 x 100
(cab) in. Those which were used in Britain were provided
there with side lights, rear mud guards, bridge plate,
camouflage paint, etc. Delivery finish was dull Coronado
tan.

TECHNICAL

The NR-5 was the same as the NR-4 tank carrier except
for the bodywork. Both had the standard Mack Lanova
diesel engine with dry-disc clutch, Duplex 10-speed
TRD37 overdrive-top transmission, drop-forged I-beam
front axle, Mack bogie with 9.02:1 double-reduction axles
and different size tyres front and rear, 11.00-24 and
14.00-20 resp. Two spares were carried, one of each size.

Top and *above:* New NR-5 readied for British service, including
Micky-Mouse camouflage paint.

Below: Example of chassis/cab as assembled in Allentown,
prior to shipment.

NR-5 and -6 Miscellany

Above: These remarkable photos show a new vehicle which has been smartened up for a special occasion: in January 1942 a new super-heavy 240-mm howitzer was hauled from Wisconsin to Aberdeen Proving Ground, via Philadelphia. The prototype NO (*qv*) and a new NR borrowed from current production were used to transport the components, the NR towing the 20-ft long barrel (on an M2 carriage, special for this purpose). The entire journey of 1,200 miles was accomplished in 11 days. This howitzer (M1) was the largest mobile artillery piece in the world, according to a report of the Philadelphia Ordnance District which was involved in the operation.

Right: Brand-new truck at Allentown ready for shipment to North Africa where these Macks (and similar Whites) moved huge tonnages of supplies to the advancing armies.

Below: Two shots of Mack NR-6 load carriers of 51 (RAF) MT Coy in the Middle East. Some clocked up more than 100,000 miles without problems on journeys to the Western Desert but also on long hauls to Lebanon and Syria (see *Wheels & Tracks* No. 39).

Mack NR-6 and -7   Truck, 10-ton, 6x4, Cargo   1942

GENERAL

In early 1942 the BPC procured a further 1,000 NRs, which were supplied in two groups, under Lend-Lease, as follows: 500 NR-6 under Contract W-670-ORD-3186 of December 17, 1941, all delivered in 1942 (British S/M2150; s/n NR4D1871D-2370D), followed by 500 NR-7 under Contract W-670-ORD-3187 of January 7, 1942, with 450 delivered in 1942, 50 in 1943 (S/M 2307; s/n NR4D2371D-2870D). The trucks were shipped PKD in single-unit packs, mostly to North Africa but unspecified batches went to other destinations: UK, India, Ceylon, West Africa, South Africa. Of 750 trucks the original USA registrations are known, i.e. 250 NR-6s: 522549-798; 500 NR-7s: 522799-3298. Known British WD Nos. were within ranges L4907091-340 and 5472753-3072. Known RAF Nos. include 89106, 100014. To complicate matters further, the US also supplied equivalent White (Model 1064) trucks under the same contracts. The Macks were valued at $9,177 apiece; the White was listed at $8,514.

PHYSICAL

Appearance similar to foregoing NRs but now with USA-pattern blackout marker lamps on front wings and stake-rack body. No Thermos water tank. Khaki paint finish. Tyre pump facility off air brake line.

TECHNICAL

Lanova diesel (Mack ED) again, TRD Duplex (2x5) OD-top gearbox, double-reduction rear axles with power divider. 11.00-24 front and 14.00-20 single rear tyres with only one spare (14.00-20). Differences between NR-6 and -7 (the latter in parentheses): rear springs with plain (anchor) ends, air brake quick-release valve on RH (LH) frame rail and wooden (diamondette) cab floor with (no) rubber mat.

Top: Chassis/cab at the factory.

Above: A portion of the NR-6s went to No. 51 (RAF) MT Company which used them often with 5-ton trailers for added load capacity.

Below: Even aircraft were carried.

Mack NR-8   Truck, 10-ton, 6x4, Cargo   1942

GENERAL

By 1942 the 10-ton Mack NR 6-wheeler had established itself, notably as a long-distance load carrier in North Africa and the Middle East and the first major modification was introduced with the NR-8, viz. a soft-top cab with half-doors and folding windscreen. Of the NR-8, 700 were built (s/n NR4D2871D-3570D). The first 150 were delivered in 1942, the remainder in 1943, all under Contract W-670-ORD-3357 of February 2, 1943, which also covered the NR-9 (qv). The initial QMC contract was W-398-QM-11597. NR-8 USA Nos. were 523299-998. Major destination was Egypt again, for the British Army and RAF. The British S/M Nos. were 2150 and 2307 (which also covered NR-6 and -7). A portion went to Australia. WD Nos. were allocated locally. The US Government valued the NR-8 at $7,840, $1,337 more than the preceding closed-cab NR-6 and -7.

PHYSICAL

With the obvious exception of the open cab with canvas folding top (like the contemporary LMSW-57 wrecker) the NR-8 looked similar to its predecessor. It measured 322 x 96 x 123 in. and weighed 42,450 lb. The cargo body's dimensions were 180 x 96 in.

TECHNICAL

Generally the same as the NR-7 but with detail differences, e.g. sealed-beam headlamps and 2-line air connections for trailer brakes. There was one spare tyre and rim for front (11.00-24) and rear (14.00-20) per vehicle. As customary there were two 75-gal. (US) fuel tanks either side of the chassis.

Top: Chassis/cab typical of NR-8 and -9. After 1,870 closed-cab NRs the open cab came at s/n NR4D2871D in late 1942.

Above: Open cab was welcomed by No. 51 (RAF) MT Coy.

Below: With 3-ton GS (Aust.) No. 2 drawbar trailer on Australia's Stuart Highway.

Mack NR-9 to -13   Truck, 10-ton, 6x4, Cargo   1943

GENERAL

The NR-9 to -13 models were supplied in large quantities during 1943-44 to the US and Allied forces: very nearly 5,000. Again, most were destined for Defense Aid and shipped under the Lend-Lease agreement to Britain as well as direct to India, North Africa (Air Ministry), Middle East, Iraq, India (Admiralty), Ceylon and Australia, where hundreds were operated on the famed outback supply routes to the Northern Territory. British order No. for the NR-10 and -11 was S/M 2432, WD registrations were within ranges 5528309-658 and 833-999, 5588703-9002 and 5824486-985. This S/M order also covered 525 White 1064s. The NR-8 and -9 were valued at $7,840, the NR-10, -11 and -12 at $8,134 and the NR-13 at £7,732 each (1944 figures). For a summary of Contract and Serial Nos. see table on following page.

PHYSICAL

NR-9 to -13 all looked the same, with open cab, single rear tyres and the US Army standard pattern wooden cargo body (180 x 88-in.) with side racks and folding seats. These bodies were supplied by The Perfection Steel Body Co. in Galion, Ohio. Some vehicles were somewhat different, with locally produced bodies.

TECHNICAL

The established technical specification was generally adhered to but there were many detail differences (often insignificant) during production and/or between contracts, especially when compared with the preceding NR-8, e.g. trailer electric connecting receptacle, fuel tanks, battery box, rear springs (13 vs 17 leaves), cab grab handles, instrument panels, pioneer tool kit, etc. In due course, as a result from rebuilds and repairs, many conformed no longer with their original specification.

Top: NR-9 carrying USA No. 524520.

Above: NR-9 to -13 three-quarter rear view, typical.

Below: British NR-10 in the Middle East.

SUMMARY OF MACK 10-TON 6X4 TRUCKS, NR-9 TO NR-13 INCL. (MODELS WITH OPEN CAB AND SINGLE REAR TYRES)

Model	Contract	Date	Quantity	Serial Nos.	USA Nos.
NR-9	W-670-ORD-3357	Feb. 2, 1943	900	NR4D3571D-4470D	523999-4898
NR-10	W-670-ORD-3351	Jan. 25, 1943	1,257	NR4D4471D-5727D	540321-1577
NR-11	W-670-ORD-4280	Feb. 22, 1943	239	NR4D5728D-5966D	544101-339
NR-12	W-670-ORD-4503	Apr. 15, 1943	1,320	NR4D5967D-7286D	5102601-3920
NR-13	W-670-ORD-5025	Aug. 30, 1943	1,280	NR4D7287D-8566D	551525-2804

Note: USA Nos. were issued for and applied to all vehicles including those which were destined for Defense Aid and shipped under the terms of the Lend-Lease agreement.

Right: Example of NR in Canadian livery, one of many stockpiled in England in 1943/44 for the coming invasion of mainland Europe.

Below left: A well-travelled NR of the British Army in post-war Germany. It is engaged in carrying Ruhr coal to RAF base Fassberg in the British Zone of occupation. Decoration and sign on radiator guard proclaim that this is the 100th load these German freight handlers are placing aboard US Air Force Skymasters of the Combined Airlift Task Force, destination Berlin: the famed Berlin Airlift of 1948-49.

Below right: Two more typical examples of mid-production Mack NR 10-tonners, this pair serving in Palestine (upper) and Australia. The Aussies called theirs the Truck, 10-ton, GS (USA). They were locally re-assembled from PKD (Partly Knocked Down) state and many were fitted with Australian GS bodies, suggesting that those were shipped from the USA in chassis/cab form.

Opposite page: 1943 advertisement, with typical artwork printed in full colour in The Saturday Evening Post.

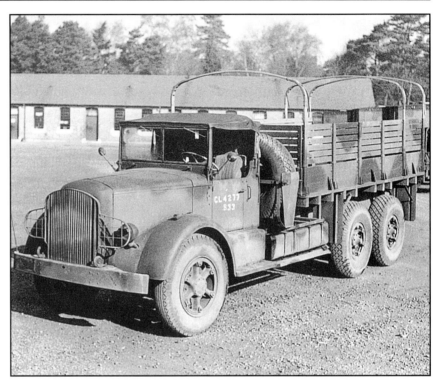

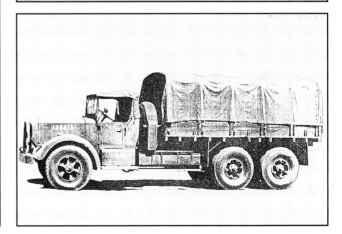

© 1943 MACK MFG. CORP.

A big 10-ton, Diesel-powered Mack in grim war paint rushes supplies to the front. Sketched from photos, by Peter Helck.

WAR REPORT...WITH A PEACETIME TWIST!...

For your future reference, we'd like to put two facts on the record now. *Fact One* —there are *more* Mack Diesels in the United Nations' armies than any other make of heavy-duty Diesel truck. *Fact Two*—the only 10-ton Diesel trucks used by United Nations' armies which are made and powered by one manufacturer are Macks. This may surprise you . . . and it may mean a lot some day when *you* are deciding what Diesel to buy.

Mack Trucks, Inc., Empire State Bldg., New York City. Factories: Allentown, Pa.; Plainfield, N.J.; New Brunswick, N. J. Factory branches and dealers in principal cities for service and parts.

IF YOU'VE GOT A MACK, YOU'RE LUCKY... IF YOU PLAN TO GET ONE, YOU'RE WISE!

Mack
TRUCKS
ONE TON TO FORTY-FIVE TONS; BUSES, FIRE APPARATUS AND MARINE ENGINES

— *BUY U. S. WAR BONDS* —

Mack NR-14 and -15   Truck, 10-ton, 6x4, Cargo   1944

GENERAL

In late 1943 the final version of the military NR chassis range was launched. It encompassed all the main features of its predecessors plus a significant characteristic of its own: dual rear tyres. The British placed an initial order (S/M 6315) for 942, soon followed by more, at least 3,150 in all. A large proportion went to India, the remainder was for Army and Air Force in Europe, including Canadian units. Total production of Mack NR-14 and -15 chassis was: NR-14 - Contract W-36-034-ORD-169 of October 16, 1943 (two batches) 7,080 trucks, s/n NR4D8567D-15646D, USA Nos. 563885-4515 and 565352-7621. NR-15 - Contract W-36-034-ORD-169 (third batch) 847 trucks, s/n NR4D15647D-16493D, USA Nos. 5103921-4767. Of the NR-14, 4,651 were supplied in 1944, 2,429 in 1945. NR-15s were all delivered in 1945 and most were probably shipped to Iran for transport of Lend-Lease material to Russia.

PHYSICAL

The NR-14 resembled the NR-9 to -13 except for the dual rear tyres, which were the same size as those up front. The body was the US Army standard wooden type, 15 x 7 ft inside and 66-in. floor-to-hoops height. The NR-15 had an entirely new body (see NR-16-20, following).

TECHNICAL

Detail improvements to engine (injection pump, oil filter, crankcase ventilation). Round military pattern dashboard instruments. Tyres 11.00-24 all round, twin rear.

Top and *above:* The first NR-14, s/n NR4D8567D, USA No. 563885, in 1944. The NR-14 was the most numerous of all NRs, accounting to nearly half of the total production so far.

Below: One of the many shipped to Britain for use by RASC and RCASC on the supply routes in Europe following D-Day.

NR-14/15
Miscellany

Above: The Canadian Army Engineers (RCE) Road Construction Units had a few Dominion 358 cranes (5/8-yd capacity) on NR-14 chassis, for general lifting and also for other work: trench hoe, dragline, clam shell and shovel equipment were supplied with each unit. The crane was made and installed on the chassis by Dominion Hoist and Shovel Co., Lachine, Quebec. The machine weighed 48,275 lb and measured 502 x 102 x 162 in.

Right: In the late 1940s the Canadian RCASC operated at least two NR-14s (and an NM) as refrigeration ration vehicles - shown here at Whitehorse, Yukon - which had been retrofitted with factory-built closed cabs, for obvious reasons.

Below: European military users after the war included Portugal (left) and Austria. Both show local modifications. The Portuguese job (possibly NR-16) has a hard cab top and a non-standard body, the Austrian one has radiator grille bars, no brush guard, lowered head lamps and a straight bumper bar. The Netherlands Army used an unknown number in the East Indies in the late 1940s. Most post-war use, however, was by civilian hauliers.

Mack NR-16 to -20   Truck, 10-ton, 6x4, Cargo   1945

GENERAL

The final model of the NR to be produced for military use was the NR-16, which was supplied under Contract 36-034-2498 (Production Order T14971). 455 had been delivered, in 1945, when the war ended; they carried s/n NR4D16494D-16948D and USA Nos. 5125021-475. The order for its successor, the NR-17, was cancelled altogether but it was not the end of the NR range yet: In late 1945 the US Treasury Department placed an order for 600 units, similar if not identical to the NR-16, for reconstruction aid to certain European countries: 150 for Belgium (NR-18, s/n NR4D16949-17098D), 150 for the Netherlands (NR-19, s/n 17099D-248D) and 300 for France (NR-20, s/n 17248D-548D). Of the earlier production types many also found their way to Europe, via the Mutual Defense Assistance Program to UN member countries. Surplus vehicles for civilian operators came mostly from British and Commonwealth stock, partly via UNRRA. Total production of NRs had reached a record 16,548.

PHYSICAL

Chassis/cab was same as NR-14 and -15, with cargo body as NR-15: all-steel with tall sides and rear doors, thus more suitable for bulk cargo haulage rather than combined cargo and personnel. NR-18 to -20 had civilian style Mack nameplates on the bonnet/hood side panels.

TECHNICAL

The technical specification of these models was the same as for their immediate predecessors.

Top: Official portrait, with canvas cover in place.

Above: In Danish Army, NR-15 or -16 supplied under MDAP in the early 1950s.

Below: End of the road for two (at least) ex-Portuguese Army.

The Belgians and French received 150 NR-18 and 300 NR-20 trucks respectively, to assist in the reconstruction of their war-torn countries. The NR-18 is shown in July 1946 in Antwerp, with original cab and lowered body; it towed a 4-wheeled trailer with a surplus original NR-18 flat-floor body. The French NR-20 (right) has more alterations: cab, body roof, low-mounted headlamps.

Dutch operators had many NRs: used ones notably from Canadian surplus (the Deelen dump contained 515, in 1946, the majority in good or repairable state) and 150 brand-new NR-19s, some of which are shown — with converted and new cabs and ditto bodies — in use by the road transport branch of the Netherlands Railways. In 1946 these Macks (with trailers) made regular journeys to Czechoslovakia, hauling various commodities. These diesel-powered trucks covered huge mileages on long-distance work.

Mack LFSW   Truck, 10-ton, 6x4, Van   1949

GENERAL

In August 1949 the US Government purchased eight LF-series Six-Wheeler chassis with extended cab. The chassis (s/n LF2D1954D-1961D) were fitted with a front-mounted winch and a van body by Charles T. Brandt, Inc., of Baltimore, Maryland. At least four were dispatched to the UK and operated there by the US Air Force as power supply vans, each with a Fruehauf 4-wheeled trailer (semi-trailers with dolly converter) fitted out as either office or stores vans. The generating sets comprised GM Diesels with 240-V 25-kVA single-phase or 75-kVA 3-phase generators, but there was also a Kohler 1.5-kVA petrol-engined unit. The four in Britain when surplussed were auctioned in January 1967 at the Ordnance Disposal Depot Hurlford in Ayrshire and ended up on an estate near Edinburgh where our photographs of the remains were taken in 1985. Their registrations included USAF 54376 and 54821.

PHYSICAL

These rare vehicles were of an unusual appearance with a very tall box van body (overall height 12 ft), an extended sleeper-type cab and a power winch at front. The sleeper cab and winch were not standard factory options for this model.

TECHNICAL

Own END405 6-cyl. diesel engine, 107 bhp at 2,200 rpm. TRD32 Duplex (5F1R x 2) transmission. SW29 tandem bogie with inter-axle differential. Westinghouse air brakes. 9.00-20 tyres, dual rear. 12-V lighting and starting.

Top: Power van with GM Diesel-driven generating set, registered USAF 54821, with winch removed.

Above: USAF 54376 with body missing and winch clearly visible.

Below: Dimensional drawing of typical LFSW with standard cab.

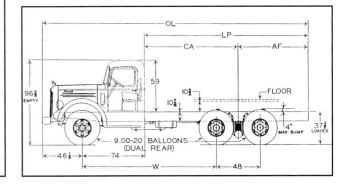

Mack LPSW   Truck, 17½-ton, 6x4, Dump   1941

GENERAL

The LP series debuted in 1941 and comprised heavy-duty
4- and 6-wheelers, replacing the 1930s' BM and BX.
Front end styling was in line with the 1940 L models. The
subject vehicle was produced in small numbers and
originally designed for the Panama Canal Third Locks
construction, where 10 were used. The British acquired
some with military features, under Contract S/M 6132.

PHYSICAL

Relatively short dump truck. Rear-tipping 12-yd body
with hoist underneath and cab protector. Open cab with
seat and windscreen for driver only.

TECHNICAL

Own 160-bhp Thermodyne petrol engine. Shaft drive to
rear axles (chassis being too short for chain drive
customary on such heavy Macks). Tyres 14.00-24 on
Budd disc wheels.

Top, *above* and *bottom right:* LPSW as supplied to Britain.

Bottom left: 6x6 version (1941) was the NW. Its driven front
axle was similar to that of the NO (*qv*). The military used some
in the Pacific on construction work.

Mack FCSW   Truck, 30-ton, 6x4, Dump   1941

GENERAL

In the late 1930s Mack offered a huge chain-drive chassis, the FC Six-Wheeler. It became well-known as an off-highway dump truck for strip mining, dam construction and such projects as the Alcan Highway. In 1941 Panama Constructors, Inc. bought 40. When in 1943 the British had a need for heavy plant for coal excavation, including dump trucks, some of these giants were acquired by the Ministry of Works under Lend-Lease terms (S/M 6157).

PHYSICAL

Long-wheelbase chassis with off-set L model cab and 25-yd rear-tipping Gar Wood dump body (20 yd water-level) with cab protector and twin hydraulic hoists.

TECHNICAL

Own 175-bhp Thermodyne driving double-reduction jackshaft through 10F2R Duplex transmission. Final drive by chains to all four rear wheels. Tyres 12.00-24 front, 14.00-24 rear. GVW 50 tons.

Top and *above:* FCSW following arrival in the UK, reassembled at a Ford Motor Co. facility.

Below: Chassis/cab in August 1944 and at work, hauling up to 32 tons.

Mack NM-1 and -2   Truck, 6-ton, 6x6, Cargo   1940

GENERAL

Mack's first military 6x6 appeared in early 1940. The QMC initially ordered 87 (Contract W-398-QM-7507, dated Dec. 9, 1939; s/n NM8D1001-1087, USA Nos. W5789-5875). They were cargo/prime mover trucks intended for hauling AA guns and crews. Unit price was $7,310. A second order followed soon, on Feb. 29, 1940: Contract 7717, for 107 units, designated NM-2 (s/n NM8D1088-1194; USA Nos. W5889-5995). These, too, were delivered in 1940. Corbitt had developed a similar model, sharing the same transfer case and axles. Mack used its newly introduced commercial L model cab. Engine and gearbox, too, were Mack's own.

PHYSICAL

Tall and stubby the NM had a winch with capstan head mounted amidships and a relatively short steel cargo body (132 x 88 in.) with troop seats and canvas cover. NM-2 had smaller headlamps with sealed-beam light units and the parking lamps mounted on top, a typical 1940 feature. Wheelbase was 177 in. (BC 52 in.). Overall dimensions 283 x 96 x 121 (cab 109) in. Weight 21,750 lb.

TECHNICAL

Own EY 6-cyl. 707-cid (5 x 6 in.) ohv petrol engine, 170 bhp at 2,100 rpm. Own TR36 5-speed direct-top gearbox. Timken-Detroit 2-speed transfer case (T77, with 2.55 low) and axles (F3100 front, with Rzeppa CV joints; SD353 rear) with double reduction. Tyres 9.75-22, highway tread (later 10.00-22). 6-Volt lighting, 12-V starting.

Top: NM-1 from the first production batch.

Above: Cargo/personnel body. Note seats, down and up.

Below: NM-2 featured separate side lamps. Photo dates from August 1940.

Mack NM-3   Truck, 6-ton, 6x6, Cargo   1941

GENERAL

In 1941 a further 104 NM-series cargo/prime mover trucks were produced under QMC Contract 8977 of Dec. 9, 1940. They carried s/n NM8D1196-1299 and USA Nos. 51762 and 52498-600. (The missing s/n 1195 belonged to a chassis that was experimentally fitted with Mack axles.) Compared with its predecessor, the NM-3 differed in several details, outlined below. It was the last of the Mack NMs with an enclosed cab, later models having the soft-top open type. The value of the NM-3 - for transfer purposes - was given as $9,406. (The NM-1 was listed at $7,448 in 1944.)

PHYSICAL

Basically similar to NM-1 and -2 but fitted with front pintle (for positioning artillery pieces) under an arched bumper; smaller brush guard; side lights now on mudguards; towing hooks above bumper deleted; radiator shell carrying Mack nameplate. Factory-installed tyres were still of the commercial type, make Lee, with highway tread.

TECHNICAL

The NM series' EY engine was a militarized version of the Mack Thermodyne EY, a big overhead-valve Six of 707 cubic inches displacement (11.6 litres). It developed 170 bhp (gross; 159 net) at 2,100 rpm and 550 lb.ft (gross; 534 net) of torque at 800 rpm. Top speed 34 mph (54 km/h). Brakes had air actuation with BW 2-cyl. compressor. Budd wheels with 22x8 rims for 10.00-22 tyres. Gar Wood US4S winch of 25,000 lb capacity.

Top: Imposing view of the NM-3, May 1941.

Above: Spares could be added to the front wheels for extra traction.

Below: The first NM-3, with all canvas in place.

NM Variants: the NN

In the NM-series chassis s/n range, which ran from NM8D-1001 to -8238, two were assigned to special projects: 1195 and 1300. Both were re-engineered to have Mack transfer case and axles, rather than the common Timken-Detroit set. The first chassis was renumbered NN8D1001 and became the Model NN-1 airport fire truck (officially: Truck, Fire, Class 150, Type O-1, 6x6, Low-Pressure Carbon Dioxide). It was produced and installed on the Mack chassis by Cardox Corp. in Chicago, to the USAAF's specific requirements and could 'quickly and effectively smother a fire by throwing thousands of pounds of carbon dioxide on a burning plane in less than three minutes'. The front and boom nozzle were both manipulated from a control panel inside the cab by means of two handles, with the control for the discharge of the CO_2 between them, as shown. The NN-1 had some civilian features like the Mack Bulldog atop the radiator. On the bonnet/hood sides it carried Cardox Airport Fire Truck name plates. Quantity production of such fire fighters was on heavy Reo and Sterling 7½-ton 6x6 chassis, shown on the right. In addition to the front and boom nozzle these airport fire trucks had front and boom foam guns, groundsweep nozzle (rigidly mounted below the front bumper) as well as fixed foam guns and hand foam guns.

Cardox Airport Fire Truck

AUG 42

RESEARCH activities at Wright Field, the Army Air Forces Materiel Center at Dayton, Ohio, have a two-fold purpose: To discover more efficient methods of destroying the enemy and to develop better means of protecting the lives of the Air Forces. As the result of two years of development work, a new life-saving device—a fire fighting truck which can quickly and effectively smother a fire by throwing thousands of pounds of carbon dioxide on a burning plane in less than three minutes—has been announced by the Equipment Laboratory of the Experimental Engineering Section there. Recently Lt. Col. Rudolph Fink, Chief of the Miscellaneous Unit of the Equipment Laboratory, and W. E. Huffman, civilian engineer, put the truck through its paces. The tests proved successful.

Developed by the Cardox Corp., Chicago, Ill., the Cardox Airport Fire Truck embodies many unique features of design, employs the characteristics of low pressure carbon dioxide systems currently used in war industries. Low pressure CO_2 is stored in large single tanks, holding from one to 25 tons of liquid carbon dioxide which is refrigerated to 0 deg. Fahr., to hold the pressure at 300 psi.

Since immediate extinguishment of crash fires on an air field is the foremost requirement of fire apparatus, the Cardox unit incorporated into its fire extinguishing technique, immediate application and mass discharge of carbon dioxide with enhanced fire extinguishing characteristics. Thus it is possible to approach an airplane crash fire with the ideal technique of fast extinguishment for the purposes of effecting rescue of the plane's crew. If the plane itself can be

(Turn to page 82, please)

Ready for approaching a crash fire, the Cardox Airport Fire Truck is shown at the right with the front nozzle pointed forward and the boom nozzle raised to position. Above it is a view of the control panel inside the cab for manipulating the nozzles and controlling the discharge of the CO_2.

The other converted NM became prototype NN-2, with s/n NN8D1002 and was delivered to the Army (Contract W-101-ORD-1137) in the beginning of 1942 with USA No. 55885. It resembled the NM-3 with the obvious exception of the axles. One more NN-2 was subsequently built, with s/n NN8D1003. By this time, the United States was at war and it was decided to standardize the 6-ton 6x6 as produced by Corbitt, White and others (with Hercules HXD 202-bhp L-head engine) for the US Army and reserve all Mack 6-ton 6x6 production for Defense Aid/Lend-Lease. The NM with Mack axles would have become the NM-4 if it had gone into production. As it was, the NM-4 never came and all subsequent production had essentially the same Timken-Detroit axles and transfer case as the NM-1 (see page 69).

Mack NM-5 and -6   Truck, 6-ton, 6x6, Cargo   1942-44

GENERAL

With the US involved directly in WWII there were changes in vehicle production and Defense Aid supplies. The NMs, now available for export, were given a soft-top cab with folding windscreen for tactical reasons and to simplify PKD shipment, saving valuable shipping space. Contract for NM-5 was W-670-ORD-3194 of Jan. 16, 1943 (previously QMC 11616 of 1942) for 1,060 units, s/n NM8D1301-2360, USA 521086-2145. They were delivered in 1942 (484) and 1943 (572), immediately followed by 3,240 NM-6s under Contract W-670-ORD-3352, dated Feb. 22, 1943, delivered 2,668 in 1943 and 572 in 1944. NM-6 s/n were NM8D2361-5600, USA 537081-540320. Main recipient was the UK with 2,382 acquired under S/M 2311 (WD H5215518, 5476128-7050, 5813958-4636 and 6228812-9067) and others shipped direct to overseas destinations.

PHYSICAL

Similar to earlier NMs but steel cab with half-doors, canvas folding top and hinged windscreen (same as on LMSW and NR models of the period) and wooden cargo body. NM-6 had rifle brackets in cab and Jerrican holders left of winch.

TECHNICAL

As before but small detail changes to engine components (pistons, oil and fuel filters, etc.), electrical equipment, dashboard (round military pattern instruments). Electric brake control (made by Warner Electric) for trailed loads. Gun-cylinder kit (as on certain Scammell artillery tractors) fitted as extra.

Top, above and *below:* General views of NM-6 as delivered ex-factory in Allentown, prior to partly dismantling for PKD shipment, July 1943.

Mack NM-7 and -8   Truck, 6-ton, 6x6, Cargo   1944-45

GENERAL

The Allies had a continuous demand for medium and heavy artillery tractors and ordered more Macks as the war drew on. Ordnance arranged further deliveries for Lend-Lease shipments to the UK and direct to destinations like the Middle East and India. The Australian, Canadian and South African forces also used NMs. The US Ordnance orders on behalf of the Allies in the final years of WWII were Contract W-670-ORD-4856 of Aug. 12, 1943, for 1,944 NM-7s (s/n NM8D5601-7544; USA Nos. 548136-550079) with deliveries of 1,174 in 1944 and 770 in 1945, followed by Contract 36-034-2423 in early 1945 for 649 NM-8s (s/n NM8D7545-8232; USA 5120283-976). It is probable that with the termination of the war the last order was curtailed and that those new trucks which were not required by the services were stockpiled. After 1945 many NMs went to various other UN member nations. In all, 7,236 NMs of all types had been produced at an average sales price of just below $8,500 apiece. How many had fallen victim to U-boats is uncertain.

PHYSICAL

The NM-7 and -8 were the same as the -5 and -6, with insignificant detail modifications during production.

TECHNICAL

As earlier models but some were equipped with the gun-carriage brake cylinder. This comprised an air-cylinder, made by Hanna Engineering Works. Its purpose was the simultaneous actuation of the truck's air brakes and the trailed gun's mechanical brakes by means of a cable. The cylinder was mounted to the right of the rear pintle hook.

Top and *above:* Typical late-production NMs, chassis/cab and with body (USA 5120868, one of the last).

Below: Gun-carriage cylinder was fitted as extra for British orders.

NM Miscellany

Top: British Army NM-5s ready for service. Many were retrofitted with round observation hatch in the canvas cab top.

Left: Hauling new Comet tanks from the Leyland works, on Rogers trailers. NMs were frequently used for towing heavy loads, on various types of trailers.

Below: Canadian-operated NM-6 (CL4275516) prime mover somewhere on the Western Front.

Bottom: The British used many NMs as recovery vehicles, mostly improvised field conversions (e.g. L5602501, left). There was also at least one chassis mounting a Coles PE revolving crane. A professional experimental twin-boom heavy breakdown tractor (L5476202, right) appeared in 1945 in prototype form but a contract for 350 - later 200 - to be built by Turner Mfg Co. was cancelled on the termination of the war.

Top: The RAF had at least 40 NMs (probably transferred from the Army) for mobile antenna equipment and used them extensively until well into the post-war period. They were classed as 10-tonners and some were passed on after the war to NATO-member countries such as France and Holland. The picture on the right shows one (51AV90) in the Middle East.

Left: Among the various wartime British NM conversions were 'artics' with ex-Albion CX24S and Scammell 'Prairie-Scooner' semi-trailers. One of them is shown, after passing from the British Army in Malaya to the Dutch in the then Netherlands East Indies, c. 1947. In 1944/45 the Army's Base Workshop in Brussels reportedly converted 15 with bolsters for logging work, using the tandem bogies from other NMs for the rear bolster which was connected by a pipe. These rigs could handle 60-ft long logs, needed for bridging operations.

Bottom: The Canadians in Europe used a long-body variant, converted by removing the winch and lengthening the standard wooden body from 11 to 15 ft. Overall length was increased by 14 in. and the resulting trucks were known as 10-ton, 6x6, GS. On the right is a post-war Canadian upgrade, comprising new Mack commercial cab, headlamps, etc. Notice also the enlarged brush guard. This example was donated to the French Army in the early 1950s.

The Austrian Bundesheer received many American vehicles, including NMs for towing 155-mm howitzers and low-bed trailers.

French NMs were mainly NM-7 and -8 (here with 90-mm AA guns), probably unused or rebuilt, plus ex-British Radar trucks.

The Dutch had standard NMs (incl. some of the latest), ex-British Radar trucks (chassis shown) and five tractors (s/n 7954 on left).

Brockway/Mack   Truck, Fire, Class 155, 6x6   1944

GENERAL

During WWII the USAAF and the Corps of Engineers introduced several new types of fire-fighting trucks, including the Class 150 Type O-1 (prototype on Mack NN-1, *qv*) and the Class 155, officially the Truck, Fire, Powered, Crash, Class 155, 6x6, High Pressure Fog Foam, dealt with here. Mack produced the first 100 of these on a variant of the Kenworth 572 chassis which was normally used for the M1 heavy wrecker. Kenworth furnished these chassis, classed as 10-ton 6x6, in 1943 under Ordnance Contract 883-3020, with USA Nos. 508023-122. Soon afterwards Ordnance procured 200 6-ton 6x6 chassis of the US Army standard type from Brockway under Contract 740-2710, for similar superstructures by both Mack and American LaFrance. They were completed and delivered in 1944 (174) and 1945 (26). Two more orders followed (Contracts 30-115-312 and -1919) for 36 and 34 respectively, in 1945.

PHYSICAL

Standard front end of the regular production types, with open cab and rectangular bodywork with two large manually-operated high-pressure nozzles on top. Overall dimensions 355 x 104 x 150 in. Weight, 31,200 lb, gross 41,700 lb. Crew six.

TECHNICAL

(Brockway) Hercules HXD 202-bhp engine, 4-speed gearbox. Timken 2-speed transfer and axles (all same as Mack NM). Continental 225-bhp engine for Hale ZEY 325-gpm pump. 1,000-gal. water and 100-gal. foam compound tank. Air brakes. 12.00-20 tyres.

Top and *above:* Brockway F666 chassis with Mack equipment.

Below: First 100 were on Kenworth chassis.

Mack NO-1   Truck, 7½-ton, 6×6, Prime Mover   1940

GENERAL

In 1940 Mack designed and constructed a prototype heavy-duty prime mover capable of handling 155-mm guns and 240-mm howitzers. Basically it was not unlike the NM with Mack axles but it had a unique elevated triple-reduction front axle, a very wide cab and a huge front winch assembly. It was procured by the US Army under Contract W-398-QM-8510 dated Sept. 27, 1940. In January 1942 this first NO model truck (s/n NO8D1001; USA registration W51556) was employed to haul the carriage of the first of the newly developed 240-mm howitzer M1 from the manufacturer - Bucyrus-Erie Co. in Milwaukee, Wisc. - to Aberdeen Proving Ground. A Mack NR (qv) was used to tow the cannon transport wagon M2, carrying the gun tube. The NO-1 was the predecessor of the 1943-45 NO-2 to -7 and the NQ (qv).

PHYSICAL

Relatively short and tall the NO had a singular appearance: a modern 6x6 chassis with an old-fashioned C-type cab (with tiny rear-hinged doors), widened to provide seating for gun crew members. Overall dimensions were 276 x 102 x 113 in. Wheelbase 155 (BC 58) in. The steel cargo body with folding troop seats measured 132 x 94 in. inside. GVW rating was 44,620 lb.

TECHNICAL

Own EY mil.-spec. petrol/gasoline 6-cyl. ohv engine, 707 cu. in. (5 x 6 in.), developing 170 bhp and driving through 5-speed direct-top gearbox combined with 2-speed transfer case. Mack axles, at front with final drive through bevel gears concentric with the king pins, dispensing with CV joints. Air brakes. Disc wheels with 12.00-24 tyres. 160-gal. (US) fuel tank.

Top and *above:* The newly completed NO-1 in December 1940.

Below: With the 240-mm howitzer carriage in tow, Wisconsin to Maryland, January 1942.

Mack NO-2   Truck, 7½-ton, 6x6, Prime Mover   1943

GENERAL

A 1942 development of the NO was the NQ (*qv*) which did not go into quantity production, unlike a revised version of the NO itself - the NO-2 - for which Mack received an order for 403 units. The contract (W-670-ORD-3303) was dated Nov. 3, 1942, the s/n range was NO8D1002-1404 and the US Army registrations were 522146-548. All were delivered in 1943. It would appear that the majority were used by the US Army, for towing heavy artillery, notably the 155-mm 'Long Tom' gun but there are indications that some were released for Defense Aid, Britain being a recipient. For transfer to other services, including international aid, the US Government assessed the NO-2, -3 and -6 at $11,830. The actual unit cost averaged $11,054.38. A total of 2,053 NOs were eventually built.

PHYSICAL

An imposing machine, not unlike the NO-1 but with major changes to front bumper and winch assembly, soft-top 4-crew cab with front-hinged doors, plain bonnet/hood sides, separate side/marker lamps on the mudguards, wooden body, etc. At the rear was a chain hoist for use when attaching 155-mm M1 gun to special drawbar and trail clamp. Wheelbase was 156 in. (BC 58 in.), overall dimensions 297 x 103 x 124 in. GVW 44,450 lb.

TECHNICAL

All major components of own manufacture: EY engine (as NM and NO-1), TRDXT36 5-speed gearbox integral with 2-speed transfer, CR38 and 39 rear axles (9.02:1), FA49 elevated front axle (overall ratio also 9.02:1). Air-actuated brakes (BW) with two air lines for gun; also Warner Electric trailer brake. Budd disc wheels with 12.00-24 tyres. Gar Wood 5MB 40,000-lb winch.

Top: USA 522544, one of the last NO-2s, May 1943.

Above: USA 522152, one of the first.

Below: Showing aperture for either standard pintle hook or special drawbar gear for M1 gun carriage.

Mack NO-3,-6,-7 Truck, 7½-ton, 6x6, Prime Mover 1943-45

GENERAL

Following the 403 NO-2s the largest order for these 'Big Macks' was also placed in 1943: Contract W-670-ORD-4290 of Feb. 2, 1943, called for a total of 1,097, all for Defense Aid, in two lots. The first group was the NO-3 with s/n NO8D1405-1501 and USA Nos. 536984-7080, all delivered in the same year. The second batch comprised the NO-6, with s/n 1504-2503, USA 544440-5439, delivered in 1943 (513) and 1944 (584). (NO-4 and -5 were special wreckers, qv.) The (final) NO-7 was delivered under Contract W-670-ORD-4858 of Aug. 31, 1943: a total of 550 (delivered 188 in 1944, 362 in 1945) with s/n 2504-3053, USA 5129823-993 and USA 550080-458. Many NO-7s, probably stockpiled in late 1945, later found their way to NATO countries like Belgium, Britain and France; Holland had a few, too. NATO also received remanufactured, rebodied earlier models.

PHYSICAL

Nearly identical to NO-2 but detail changes e.g. universal rifle bracket, key-less ignition switch, battery tray vs box. From NO-6 different spare wheel carrier, door curtains, front mudguard tread plates, winch cable (with Fiege eye, shackle and hook vs thimble and hook), steering gear and clutch pedals on fabricated vs cast bracket, revised fuel tank filler spout. The bodies were supplied by a local firm, Schantz Furniture Co.

TECHNICAL

The NO-3, -6 and -7 as produced during 1943-45 were similar in all major respects to the preceding NO-2.

Top: NO-6 with machine gun ring mount.

Above: Macks on tour in a War Bonds drive.

Below: NO-6 ready for British Army service. Notice the single headlamp, located further forward.

Above left: Jeep and Big Mack in comparison view with only the headlamps being about the same size.
Above right: NO at final inspection with Bob Fritzges in charge, 1943.

Right: The most notable feature of the NO (and some other Macks) was the 'elevated' front axle which did away with drive shaft joints in the steering ends.

Below: In-cab and chassis views of this remarkable Mack, in the summer of 1943. Basically the huge NO had the same drive line layout as the US Army's smaller (1½- to 6-ton) six-wheel drive trucks.

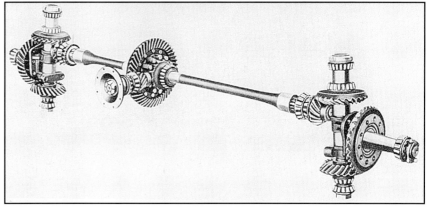

The NO was the only Mack tactical truck to be used fairly extensively by the US Army, mainly for towing 155-mm M1 'Long Tom' guns during the Italian campaign and in the ETO following D-Day. Drivers disliked the road shock kickback through its steering.

Mack NOs in action in the Lu Selva area, Italy, Jan. 19, 1944 (above) and in France, en route to Brest, exactly seven months later.

NOs in Foreign Service

The British had NOs during WWII (above left) and in the 1950s received more, now rebuilt (most if not all by Corbitt) steel-bodied ones (right) for towing heavy guns and later also plant trailers (below) at home and in Germany (BAOR; British Army of the Rhine).

Below: The post-war Belgian Army had nearly 200, 70 with new coachbuilt cab (left); the Dutch received 10 (right), all under the Mutual Defense Assistance Program (MDAP), which from the early 1960s was renamed Military Assistance Program (MAP).

On December 14, 1942, the US Ordnance Department awarded Mack an order (Contract W-670-ORD-3699) for two prototype heavy wreckers on modified NO chassis: one for the US Army Air Forces (NO-4; s/n NO8D1502) and one for the Field Artillery (NO-5; s/n NO8D1503). Both were built on long-wheelbase chassis variants with the winch moved to the rear and with a Gar Wood single-boom slewing crane. Wheelbase was 227 in., overall length, width and height 372 x 102 x 126 in.

The NO-4 had a fifth-wheel coupling for aircraft recovery semi-trailers (like the USAAF's C2 wreckers) and weighed 38,450 lb. The photos were taken on completion of the vehicles in April and May of 1943.

The NO-5 (opposite page) was equipped with an extra recovery winch mounted just ahead of a small platform with low removable boards. It weighed 41,210 lb. Payload was 10,000 lb. Both units had facilities for winching at the front via cable guides. When testing had taken place it was decided not to go ahead with either project and the two wreckers were assigned for facility use. (See also *Wheels & Tracks* No. 14.)

NO-4 and -5 Heavy Wreckers

Like the NO-2, -3, -6 and -7 prime movers, both the NO-4 and -5 featured a special drawbar for towing certain Ordnance trailers and gun carriages by means of a trail clamp. This drawbar was interchangeable with the standard US Army type pintle hook, which could then be carried under the body. The heavy trail clamp and drawbar assembly —

also known as the Mack coupler — was handled by the chain hoist on the prime movers and by the crane on the wreckers. Thus, the NO-4 was capable of towing conventional semi-trailers as well as Ordnance specials like the one shown (another had four wheels, in tandem, with 14.00-20 tyres and wide track, for transport of Engineers equipment).

Mack NO/Northwest Crane Carrier

Even more unusual than the NO-4 and -5 heavy wreckers was the crane carrier conversion of an unknown quantity of Mack NO chassis in the late 1940s or early '50s. As the heading photo shows the entire chassis frame was new, with deep side rails and substantial outriggers ahead of and behind the tandem bogie. At least one such machine was supplied via Military Assistance in the 1950s to the British Royal Navy. It carried a revolving crane manufactured by Northwest Engineering Co. of Chicago, Illinois. An enclosed half-cab replaced the full-width original. The crane had a lattice-type boom and could be used also as a dragline, clamshell and pile driver. A separate diesel engine was mounted in the crane body. The example shown below carried Royal Navy registration 38RN70 and was eventually auctioned at Ruddington as Mobile Crane, 12-ton, 6x6 in October 1966. (The Royal Navy also had at least one rebuilt standard Mack NO, registered 12RN14; this vehicle was sold at Ruddington in December 1974, for £700.)

Northwest cranes produced for the US Army in WWII were mainly the Shovel, Crawler-mounted, Diesel Engine-driven, 2-cu.yd, Northwest 78D, for the Corps of Engineers. As a crane they could lift 21 tons with 50-ft boom at 15-ft radius.

MACK NQ   Truck, Prime Mover, Heavy, T15, T16   1942

GENERAL

Among the largest military trucks produced by Mack in WWII were the heavy prime movers T15 (with cargo body and pintle for full trailing loads) and the T16 (with fifth-wheel for semi-trailers). They were built in 1942 under Contract W-670-ORD-1842, with s/n NQ8D1001-1003 and USA Nos. W55280-82. Very similar to the Mack NO-1 (*qv*) these units were intended for transporting the 240-mm howitzer M1. The one with USA No. W55280 appeared both with cargo body (as T15) and with fifth-wheel coupling (as T16), so all three could be used to tow semi-trailers which likewise were specially designed and built, by Mack: the T29 for the gun tube or barrel, the T30 for the gun carriage and the T31 to carry crew and ammunition. The M1 howitzer fired the heaviest projectile of any US Army field artillery weapon: it weighed 360 lb. The 38-ton High-speed tractor M6 became the standard prime mover for this piece.

PHYSICAL

Similar to the NO-1 (including the ancient C-type cab) but 14.00-24 tyres and side/marker lamps positioned on the front mudguards rather than atop the headlamps. The T15 measured 276 x 116.5 x 123 in., the T16 273 x 113 x 116 in. Wheelbase was 157 (BC 58) in. The third vehicle (s/n 1003) had a second winch behind the cab. The weight was 27,050 lb, gross 54,810 lb; GTW rating was 60,000 lb.

TECHNICAL

Engine and power train same as NO except that the front axle was heavier and the overall gear ratio of all axles was lower at 10.75 vs 9.02:1 to compensate for the larger tyres. Max. speed was 28 mph; range 350 miles.

Top and *above:* NQ s/n 1001 with cargo/prime mover body, designated T15. (T for experimental vehicle.)

Below: The T15 from the rear, showing USA No. W55280.

Various early-1942 views of the T16s: NQ8D1001/USA W55280 with spare wheel and NQ8D1003/USA W55282 with extra winch.

Special Mack semi-trailers T29, T30 and T31 (USA 0107761-763). T31 was ammunition and crew carrier. Note its overhead hoist.

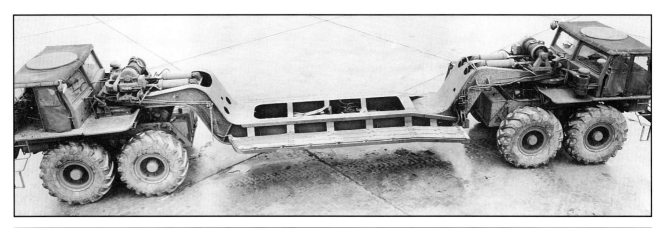

Mack T8   Tank Transporter, 8x8, T8   1945

GENERAL

Early in WWII the US Army for the first time defined an off-road capability for a new tank transporter. After several ideas had been explored the basic concept of a so-called double-ender was conceived in 1942. It was a transporter utilizing two wheeled tractor units with the load suspended between them. A test rig comprising single-axle units at both ends was constructed by LeTourneau and designated T4. In order to reduce axle loadings and surmount other shortcomings, this concept was further refined and a new prototype was designed, called the T8 of which three were produced by Mack and tested extensively at APG. It never reached quantity production, however, as it completed its tests only shortly before the war's end.

PHYSICAL

The T8 double-ender comprised two 4x4 tractor units, as shown; one pulling, one pushing. It could lower its centre platform for (un)loading, i.e. at the rear end. Overall dimensions 713 x 124 x 132 in. Wheelbase 76 + 426 + 76 in. Track 101 in. Ground clearance under platform 35 in., under axles 20 in. Weight 99,100 lb; payload limited to 35 tons, equally divided over the eight wheels. Crew five.

TECHNICAL

Two Hall-Scott 440/441 6-cyl. 1090-cu.in. ohv petrol/gasoline engines, each developing 240 bhp at 2,000 rpm. Each engine driving two axles through Spicer 3F1R torque converter transmissions. Controlled-diff. steering. Air brakes. Walking-beam suspension. 21.00-28/24-ply deeply-cleated M&S tyres with directional tread. Turning radius 42.5 ft. Two 30-ton winches. Fuel capacity 200 gal.

Top(2): T8 No. 1 facing left and, uncoupled, facing right.

Above: Test-loaded with Pershing medium tank, M26.

Below: Three-quarter front view, with stake racks, Aug. 1945.

T8E1 and T9 Double-Enders

The second tank and heavy equipment transporter of the T8 double-ender concept was the T8E1 (USA registration 5137225). It was similar to the first, with the main exception of being much more powerful: the two 240-bhp Hall-Scott in-line Sixes had made way for a pair of the famed Ford GAA tank engines, the big V8s of 1100-cu.in. displacement (5.4 x 6-in. bore and stroke) which each turned out 450 bhp (net) at 2,600 rpm and 950 lb.ft of torque at 2,100, i.e. a combined power output of 900 bhp (net; 1000 gross) for the complete rig, which now weighed 92,400 lb and with 21.00-29 tyres could carry 40 tons. The T8E1 is shown above and on the right during tests at Aberdeen Proving Ground where all manner of loads were carried. Shown are Sherman (top) and T23 medium tanks in 1945 and an M44 armoured utility vehicle in 1946. To tell the front from the rear, notice the sloping ends of the platform runways, which are at the rear.

A further development of the 'wheeled bridges' was the experimental T9 of 1950. Mack had produced three T8s, in 1945-46, and this was probably a reworked T8E1. The T9 carried the huge 280-mm gun, as shown (below) and was 71 ft long.

The double-ender concept was revived later in the 1950s, with two 8x8 end units for which Mack supplied the axles (*qv*).

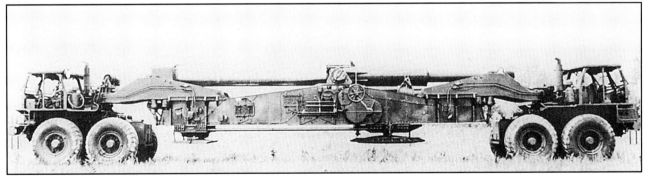

Mack T3   Truck, Half-Track, T3   1941

GENERAL

As early as 1940 the US Army Ordnance Committee
studied proposals for a better half-track vehicle, with
longer tracks than the scout car-derived models which
had just been standardized. A prototype half-track truck
chassis (also known as ¾-Track) was ordered from Mack
in December 1940. Designated T3 this half-track chassis
was actually delivered with an armour-plate hull, in
October 1941. It was intended to be used for several
roles, notably as a prime mover for the 105-mm
howitzer. The chassis was similar in some respects to
contemporary German designs, i.e. long tracks with
individual steering brakes and a non-driving front axle.
Tests showed various shortcomings which could be, but
were not, rectified. The chassis was used temporarily for
an AA gun motor carriage (see following page) but later
converted back to its original configuration.

PHYSICAL

Open-top armoured hull, seating 10 crew in APC form.
Side doors to cab area. Forward control, with engine at
rear. Vertical volute-spring suspension units from M2
light tank, two on either side. Steel bogie wheels (later
rubber-tyred) and tracks with rubber blocks. Overall 245
x 77 x 72 in. Net weight 20,720 lb.

TECHNICAL

Mack EY 707-cid truck engine at rear with twin
carburettors, developing 192 bhp, driving midship-
mounted 2-speed auxiliary gearbox via 5F1R
transmission. Controlled differential with air-actuated
brakes for each track, linked to the front wheel steering
system. Tank-type suspension and tracks with rubber
bushings. 14-ton winch up front.

Above and *below:* T3 with armour-plate hull.

Top: Preserved at APG, c. 1949 (MCV120), minus front bumper.
Notice rubber-tyred bogie wheels.

Above: T3 and chassis as used for the T1 gun carrier.

Below: Experimental 40-mm (Bofors) AA gun motor carriage, T1, with Kerrison gun director, photographed at Aberdeen Proving Ground, Maryland, on December 8, 1941.

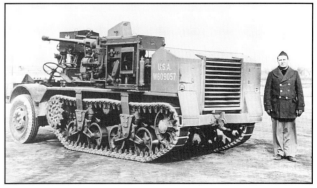

Mack T19   Truck, Half-Track, T19   1942

GENERAL

In 1942 the Ordnance Department planned several new half- or three-quarter-tracked trucks, designated T16 to T19. Of the T18 and T19 two prototypes each were to be built by Mack, but the T18 was soon dropped. For the T19 (which was similar except for having a petrol engine instead of a diesel) Mack received a contract (W-670-ORD-2159) in early April. The first vehicle was delivered in November of the same year, the other in April 1943. The T19 looked like the earlier T3 but had different suspension and many detail alterations. The two prototypes, which during tests were further improved in various respects, were numbered USA W4015647 and 648. Their proposed use, if accepted, would have been prime mover for the 105-mm howitzer with armour protection for the crew, or/and as a 14-seat personnel carrier.

PHYSICAL

Generally similar to the 1941 T3 but with many detail differences, including deletion of the access doors. It measured 247 x 101 x 86 (hull) in., weighed 23,292 lb (combat-loaded 28,800 lb.) and could accommodate a 14-member crew plus kit. The hull armour was ¼-in. thick. Engine (at rear) same as M5 high-speed full-track tractor.

TECHNICAL

Continental R6572 6-cyl. 215-bhp (net) 572-cid ohv petrol/gasoline engine with Lipe clutch and Mack 4F1R synchromesh transmission and 2-speed transfer case. Controlled differential to assist steering, with contracting-band brakes on jackshaft. Centre-pivot equalized suspension with light tank tracks. Front tyres 9.00-20. Maximum speed 38 mph. Winch capacity 15,000 lb.

Top and *above:* T19 No. 1, as seen at APG in late 1942.

Below: Winch was mounted off-centre in the bow.

T19s USA W4015648 and 647 as tested, the latter by the Armored Board (following trials by the Field Artillery Board) in 1943.

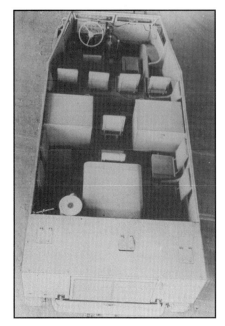

T19 at Fort Knox with 'competitors' T16 (by Diamond T) and T17 (by White). The T16 carried USA registration W4015650.

Instrument Carrier, T18

Mack's only involvement with the US Army's standardized half-tracks was the modification of a pair of M3s in early 1943 to carry the M5 fire director, the computing instrument (and power unit) serving as fire-control mechanism for the T59 40-mm gun motor carriage, also on a converted half-track. This was a single-barrel Bofors anti-aircraft gun. The T18's hull had been extended upwards and the M5 director was mounted on a tripod. The vehicles remained experimental. One T18 survived the war, at least until the late 1940s, at APG (MCV298), only to be disposed of shortly afterwards, along with the various half-track trucks (T3, T9, T17, T19) and many others. Most if not all of these experimental vehicles fell victim to the cutting torch.

The standardized half-tracks were products of White, Autocar and Diamond T, using a White 6-cyl. L-head engine, Spicer transmission and transfer case, Timken-Detroit front and rear axles. A typical M3 measured 235 (w/o winch) × 87.5 × 89 in.

97

In addition to motor vehicles, Mack Manufacturing Corp. produced other war materials, including transmissions for medium tanks. When the US War Department placed its first orders for M3 medium tanks, Mack was contracted for transmissions: power trains comprising 5-speed gearbox with differential and final drives. There were three Ordnance contracts for M3 units, during 1941-42, totalling 2,302. The first contract for transmissions for the M4 Sherman came in June 1941: 500 units, followed by 1,130 for Baldwin Locomotive (1942) and 650 for Pullman Standard (1942-43). In addition, 350 were supplied to other users (Britain and Canada). They were manufactured in Mack's New Brunswick, NJ, gear plant, which had been enlarged for this work. Total tank transmission business reached nearly $40 million.

Illustrated are *(left)* the cutting of driving gears; a period advertisement *(below left),* which appeared also with alternative text ('more than 300 times the weight of a passenger car transmission', etc.); a typical complete assembly being installed in an early M4 Sherman *(below)* and *(bottom)* the nameplate 'Mack Medium M3 Power Train' visible in a Canadian-built Ram tank.

The gearbox/transmission's gear ratios were 7.56, 3.11, 1.78, 1.11, 0.733 and reverse 5.65:1. All except low and reverse had synchromesh engagement. Oil capacity was 26 qt for the gearbox, 120 for the diff/final drive.

Mack   Tank Transmissions, M3, M4   1941-43

Mack LR　　Truck, 15-ton, 4x2, Dump　　1952

GENERAL

In 1952/53 the US Army and Air Force procured numbers of Mack LR off-road chassis with 10-yd rear dump bodies supplied by Heil or Marion Metal Products, under model designation RB100. Twin, double-acting 8-in. diameter hydraulic cylinders with 24-in. stroke provided 70° dumping angle, with power return. They were near-standard commercial trucks, used primarily for quarry, mine and road building operations. Similar heavy-duty dump trucks were supplied to the US Army by Euclid, in various types (Models 4FD, 5FD, etc.). The LR was among the first new commercial Macks supplied to the military after World War II.

PHYSICAL

Large dumper of conventional appearance with relatively short body. Closed cab, Model CA18, offset 10¾-in. to the left providing driver's vision around the truck body. Heavy channel-type front bumper with wood filler. Rock-type body with scoop end. Body inside dimensions 158 x 120 in. Capacity 10 cubic yards. Wheelbase 160 in. Overall dimensions 300 x 129 x 130 in. Weight 37,500 lb.

TECHNICAL

Cummins NHB600 6-cyl. 743-cid diesel engine, 200 bhp at 2,100 rpm. Mack TRDX510 two-lever Duplex 8F2R overdrive-top transmission. Mack Planidrive rear axle with overall ratio of 19.40:1 (carrier 5.38, planetary 3.60:1). Air brakes. Cast spoke wheels with 14.00-24 tyres.

Top: USA 5179041, s/n LR1S1362D, official portrait dated October 1952.

Above: Three-quarter rear view as appeared in manual ENG7&8-3476 of May 1956.

Below: Demobbed in Europe, late 1970s.

Miscellaneous Post-WWII 4x2

In the post-war years various countries around the world invested in commercial-type Mack trucks for military use. Some were specially adapted to meet stringent requirements, others were virtually 'standard', i.e. assembled from off-the-shelf components which always included numerous options. Shown are some typical 4x2 models.

In the mid-1970s Mack received a large military fleet order from an undisclosed African country, Nigeria most likely. It comprised several 4x2 and 6x4 models from the DM and R 600 Series, both of which had been introduced in the 1960s.

The DMs (400/600 Series) 4x2 and 6x4 were basically construction trucks (for dumpers, mixers, etc.) and had an off-set cab, a short front axle-to-back-of-cab dimension and choice of unitized GRP (plastic) front end or steel butterfly-type bonnet/hood. Engines ranged from 180 to 375 bhp. The R Series 4x2 and 6x4 had GVW ratings from 27,500 to 56,000 lb and also a wide range of engine options (including Mack/Scania diesels) from 155 to 375 bhp. Illustrated on this page are some models of the African order, i.e. a DM600X tanker (above), an R600T Holmes-equipped wrecker (with Model 600 twin-boom medium wrecker and body furnished by Ernest Holmes Export Corp.) and a schoolbus-type personnel carrier, also on the R600T chassis.

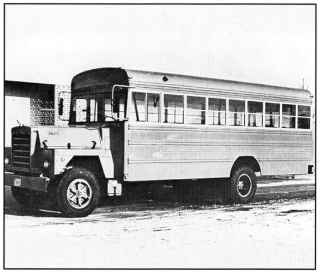

Above left: MB-series tilt-cab short-haul tractor — Model MB410 — with own EN414A V8 petrol engine, 11.00-20 tyres and 'up to 45° wheelcut' for tight turns; one of a number used by the US Navy, notably in Japan, from 1966 until 1976. Typical registration USN96-29126. *On the right* is its successor, the MC400P-series Low Cab Forward of the late 1970s, with 175-bhp Caterpillar 3208DI V8 diesel and 9.00-20 tyres.

Left: Sign of recent times. In 1983 Renault V.I. (Véhicules Industriels) acquired a controlling interest in Mack and since then there has been extensive cooperation. In its Blainville factory RVI produced a range of Mid-Liner medium trucks which are badged Mack for sale in the USA as the MS Series with choice of major components, wheelbase sizes, etc. Shown is a US Air Force 1990 Mid-Liner at Rhein Main AFB in Germany, carrying liquid nitrogen.

Below: In the 1960s Mack had launched a new series of off-highway end dumpers, ranging from the M15X 15-tonner (which replaced the LR, *qv*) up to a 75-ton 6x4 (M75SX) with self-steering bogie. In due course the military invested in small quantities of the M15X and M20X, both with 155-in. wheelbase and 14.00-25 tyres. Power train was all Mack, with Planidrive rear axle, but the M20X could be supplied also with Cummins and Detroit Diesel engine and it had 16.00-25 tyres at the rear. A US Army M15X with 11-cu. yd body is shown on the left and on the right a 20-ton M20X with 13-cu. yd body can be seen as operated by the US Navy in the mid-1970s.

Mack B-Series   Trucks, 6x4, Tractor   1955

GENERAL

Launched in 1953 the B-series heavy-duty Macks were restyled models available in GVW ratings of 17,000 for the B20 to 65,000 lb for the B71. The B42 was the most numerous, with nearly 47,500 built until 1966. During those years many variants were added and the lists of options were extensive. Many Mack fans consider the B to be one of the best looking trucks ever built by the Allentown plant. They were available in 4x2 and 6x4 configuration for highway and 'straight truck' use but there were also 6x6 models and off-road chassis with Mack's own Tri-axle bogie. It would appear that the US Navy was the principal military customer, known examples including B70ST and B71ST 6x4 tractor trucks in 1955 and long (222.5-in. wheelbase) B71S 10-ton stake trucks (s/n B71S1306, 1308) in the same year, the latter costing $11,142.

PHYSICAL

Rounded nose, mudguards and cab on most, but square-style front ends were optional on certain models. Typical Mack cast-spoke wheels with 20- or 22-in. rims and various tyres sizes.

TECHNICAL

Typical B71S specification (US Navy): Cummins 6-cyl. diesel engine with power output of 200 bhp at 2,100 rpm, driving tandem axles via Mack 5-speed manual transmission. Tyres 11.00-20. Air brakes.

Top: B71ST (s/n 1316) as delivered to the US Navy in September 1955.

Above: B70ST (s/n 1319), supplied in November 1955, also to the US Navy.

Below: Flat-nose B75 hauling Super Sabre with rocket take-off equipment on mobile launcher, early 1960s.

Mack R611ST   Truck, 6x4, Tractor   1977

GENERAL

Mack's R-series trucks first appeared in 1965 and were advertised as 'the Workhorse of the Highway'. They were offered in a range of 27,500 to 56,000 lb GVW ratings and became a familiar sight 'stateside and off-shore'. Powertrains were available with up to 375 bhp, by Mack and other manaufacturers. The all-steel cab had a cockpit-style wraparound console for its instruments and dash-mounted controls. In addition to the US Army and Air Force there were other military customers, notably in Africa and Asia. Military R-series Macks hardly differed from their civilian counterparts. The R611ST tractors shown reportedly cost $51,693 each. Typical USAF registrations: 77B1149-1159.

PHYSICAL

R-series Macks looked much like the DM of comparable size. The tractor units had the cab mounted in the centre, rather than off-set to the left as customary on certain other models (e.g. the DM and U models). Overall dimensions 228 x 95 x 105 in.

TECHNICAL

Own ENDT 673 6-cyl. diesel engine, developing 225 bhp (260 gross) at 2,100 rpm. TRD722 5F1Rx2 direct-top Duplex transmission. SWS56C double-drive tandem bogie. Air brakes. Cast-spoke wheels with 10.00-20 tyres. Wheelbase 151 (BC 50) in. 24-Volt electrical equipment.

Top: USAF 77B1153 with box van semi-trailer at a US Air Force base in Germany, c. 1980.

Above: USAF 77B1156 (s/n 21656) demobbed in Europe.

Below: USAF 77B1154, new in April 1977, as seen in October 1985.

Mack DM492S   Truck, 15-ton, 6x4, Refueler   1980

GENERAL

In 1980 Mack Trucks received a Government contract for delivery of over 1,000 chassis/cabs for aircraft refueler chassis for the US Air Force. They were long-wheelbase conventionals with forward-tilting bonnet/hood-cum-mudguards/fenders assembly made of GRP (glassfibre-reinforced plastic) as introduced on the R series trucks in 1965. The tanks - which could hold 5,000 US gallons - and the pumping equipment were made and installed by two sub-contractors, i.e. Condiesel Mobile Equipment and Kovatch Corp. of Nesquehoning, Pennsylvania. The vehicles cost around $82,000 apiece and were delivered as follows: 180 units in 1981, 420 in 1982 and 410 in 1983, totalling 1,010 units. They were used on US Air Force bases at home and overseas until well into the 1990s.

PHYSICAL

Exceptionally long vehicle with conventional but off-set cab with behind it the pumping equipment compartment and the large 5,000-gal. tank for JP4 jet fuel and possibly other liquids. The exhaust silencer/muffler was located below the front bumper.

TECHNICAL

Caterpillar 3208 V8-cylinder 636-cid diesel engine, developing 210 bhp at 2,800 rpm. GM Allison automatic transmission. Double drive tandem bogie. Air-actuated brakes. Cast-spoke wheels with 11.00-20 tyres, dual rear, on demountable rims.

Top and *above:* USAF 81L117, with Kovatch equipment, stationed at Soesterberg Air Force Base in Holland, mid-1980s.

Below: Condiesel-equipped example at Ramstein AFB in Germany, 1981.

Shown on these pages are additional examples of Mack 6x4 trucks for military use in the post-war years, notably derivatives of commercial models of the 1970s and '80s.

Post-WWII 6x4 Miscellany

Above: Heavy Equipment Transporter (HET) of the South African Defence Force, a Mack RD-series 6x4 with 4-axle semi-trailer in the early 1980s. Polyester unitized front end was standard; steel butterfly type hood was optional.

Right: R685ST with tandem-axle semi-trailer of the Israeli Defence Force, 1983. Many were used for road haulage.

Below: RD600-series 6x4s of the US Government serving as water tanker and with 'reefer' (refrigerated van) semi-trailer with the Multinational Force and Observers (MFO) in the Sinai, early 1980s.

Above: R685ST 6×4 chassis (s/n 60176) with Holmes 750 twin-boom heavy wrecker equipment delivered to an undisclosed African military customer in 1977.

Mack's most important African army clients in the 1970s were Nigeria and South Africa. The latter country in the mid and late 1970s and early 1980s acquired several batches of heavy-duty recovery vehicles, 6×6, and sizable tank-transporter tractors, 6×4 and 6×6 (e.g. R795 tractors and RM6866 with RF66 semi-trailers) for hauling Olifant (Centurion) MBTs and other loads of up to 60 tons.

Below: 1970s' DM600-series long-wheelbase chassis/cab bodied as aircraft refueller and (right) as an extra-long cargo carrier. The refueller (by RAMTA Division of Israel Aircraft Industries) had a wheelbase of 237 in. and measured 366 x 98 x 126 in. overall. It had a 17,000-litre tank and a 300-gpm pump.

Bottom: DM685S truck and ST tractor for African client in the mid-1970s. The US Air Force had DM600-series 10-ton 6×4 chassis (with Maxitorque 6-cyl. diesel) carrying a 12-15-yd dump body, serving the USAF Civil Engineering Battalions.

A selection of DM800-series units, custom-built and delivered in the 1970s and early '80s. The tractor units above and right (with disc wheels) went to the US Navy in 1980-84. The chassis/cab below right is a DM885SX, in which '85' (second and third digits) indicated the 237-bhp Mack ENDT675 6-cyl. engine. Below left is a DM895SX with 280-bhp ENDDT865, as supplied in quantity to Israel. All have set-back front axle, off-set cab, steel butterfly-type bonnet/hood and tilt mudguards for walk-in engine accessibility. Each Mack was custom-built, whereby the client had choice of numerous options. Notice, for example, the differences in wheelbase and tyre sizes here and the fitment of a sleeper box, cab roof heat shield, cage over winch, radiator guard and other features on the different models.

Above: Positively huge was the cab-over engine F897ST of 1973, with a GVW rating of 102,000 lb. It was tested by the US Army with HET semi-trailers but not adopted. This impressive machine had a 375-bhp ENDT866 V8 diesel engine with 12F5R transmission. Tyres were 14.00-24. A 6x6 variant was produced and tested also (*qv*).

Left: In 1990/91 these MR600S-series refuellers were supplied to the Bahrain Defence Force. The 18,200-litre tanks and pumping equipment were furnished by ADE HML Ltd of Middlesex, England.

Below: White and shiny Ultra-Liner of the US Army Recruiting Command, snapped at Ft Knox, Kentucky in the early '90s.

Mack T54   Truck, 5-ton, 6x6, Cargo, T54   1950

GENERAL

In the late 1940s the US Army Ordnance Department experimented with a whole new family of tactical vehicles of many sorts, wheeled and tracked. There were many highly sophisticated designs, intended to be great improvements on the WWII fleet, incorporating all the lessons learned, and more. As early as 1947 Mack was entrusted with the engineering and development of a refined 5-ton 6x6 truck, officially designated Carrier, Cross-Country, 5-ton, 6x6, T54. Two prototypes were built, one with aluminium cargo body, the other with a steel one. Both had an aluminium cab. The T54 was tested simultaneously with what became the standardized M-series 5-ton 6x6 (following page), but rejected.

PHYSICAL

Angular appearance, with rounded mudguards and six single-tyres wheels, sloping alligator-type bonnet/hood and cargo body with long wheel-wells. The body had no fewer than 11 top bows. Wheelbase 155 in. Overall 286 x 96 x 122 (min. 88) in. Weight 18,450 (w/steel body 19,600) lb.

TECHNICAL

Continental OA-536-1 horizontally-opposed 6-cyl. air-cooled petrol engine with magneto ignition. Power output 180 bhp approx. Allison TT270 torque converter with automatic transmission. Single-speed transfer. Independent front suspension with torsion bars; leaf springs and walking beams at rear. Central tyre inflation system. Tyre size 14.00-20. 10-ton Tulsa winch at front.

Top and *above:* Prototype No. 1, with aluminium cab and body, in November 1950.

Below: No. 2 had a steel cargo body and USA No. 5159769.

Mack M51   Truck, 5-ton, 6x6, Dump, M51   1952

GENERAL

At the time of the Korean War the US Army standardized a range of newly developed 6x6 tactical trucks: 2½-, 5- and 10-tonners with various body types. The 5-ton model had been pioneered by International Harvester, in conjunction with Ordnance. Initially International, Diamond T and Mack were contracted for volume production: Cargo M41 and M54, Dump M51, Tractor M52, Wrecker M62 and chassis/cabs for special applications M40, M61 and M139. The vehicles' mechanical components were identical and supplied by the same sub-contractors. There were differences in wheelbase lengths, tyres sizes. Most had a front-mounted winch, by Gar Wood. Mack-built M51s had s/n M51M1001 onwards. The basic design remained current for decades.

PHYSICAL

Similar appearance to the more common M-series 2½-ton 6x6 but flat radiator grille, 10-stud wheels and front axle further forward in relation to mudguards. Steel 5.5-yd dump body (floor 125 x 82 in.) with cab protector. Wheelbase 167 (BC 54) in. Overall 282 x 97 x 110 (min. 88) in. Weight 22,664 lb. (All with winch.)

TECHNICAL

Continental R6602 6-cyl. 602-cid 196-bhp (net, at 2,800 rpm) ohv petrol engine. Spicer 6352 5-speed direct-top synchromesh gearbox. 2-speed transfer case with automatic front drive engagement. Double-reduction axles, ratio 6.43:1. Air-over-hydraulic brakes. 11.00-20 tyres. Winch capacity 10 tons.

Top: New Mack-built M51 dump truck.

Above: Three-quarter rear view; body by Marion.

Below: Demobbed USAF 52K22592, built in 1952.

Mack M52 Truck, 5-ton, 6x6, Tractor, M52(A1) 1952('62)

GENERAL

Among the earliest versions of the US Army's M-series
5-ton 6x6 range was the tractor truck for semi-trailers,
the M52. It was supplied also to the USAF, usually with
the optional hard-top cab. In the early 1960s it was
decided to 'dieselize' the M52 tractor and the M54 cargo
truck fleet to provide greater fuel economy. Commercial
diesel engines from Cummins and Mack were tried. The
Mack ENDT673 was selected and new trucks with this
engine received the suffix A1 to their model code. Mack
supplied these power units also for vehicles asssembled
by other contractors and it applied to more models than
the initial M52A1 and M54A1 in 1962. Only just over
2,500 were built, though, because within two years the
Continental- and Hercules-built multi-fuel engines were
standardized instead.

PHYSICAL

Outward appearance was as dump truck (qv) but with
fifth-wheel coupling for semi-trailers, including deck
plate, trailer brake hoses and connections. Overall
dimensions 257.5 x 97 x 103 in. Weight 18,313 lb.
(Winch-equipped M52s were 15.5 in. longer and 715 lb
heavier.)

TECHNICAL

M52: see preceding page. M52A1: Mack ENDT673 6-cyl.
turbocharged diesel engine, 205 bhp (net) at 2,100 rpm,
with Rockford 15TN clutch and Spicer 6453 5-speed
overdrive-top gearbox.

Top: Early tractor truck, without winch.

Above: M52 on active duty in Japan, 1960s.

Below: With 12-ton M127 semi-trailers.

Mack was contracted for several 5-ton 6x6 model variants, notably the M54 cargo truck and the long M55 ditto (below) which had 215-in. wheelbase and 244-in. long body (vs 179 and 168 in. resp. for M54 cargo truck); the M61 chassis for water distributor (left; 1,000-gal. Model 73) and the M139C and M139D chassis for rocket launchers (bottom; 762-mm 'Honest John' M289 and M386 resp.).

Many M-series 5-ton 6x6 trucks of various types were exported to NATO and other 'friendly' nations throughout the Cold War period and the trucks' overall appearance changed but little until the 1980s when the 'big nose' M939 range appeared.

Opposite page: The M54E3 was the prototype M54 cargo truck, 5-ton, 6x6, with Mack ENDT673 turbocharged diesel engine (M54A1), shown below. It developed 211 bhp (gross) at 2,100 rpm.

Mack-built M-series Miscellany

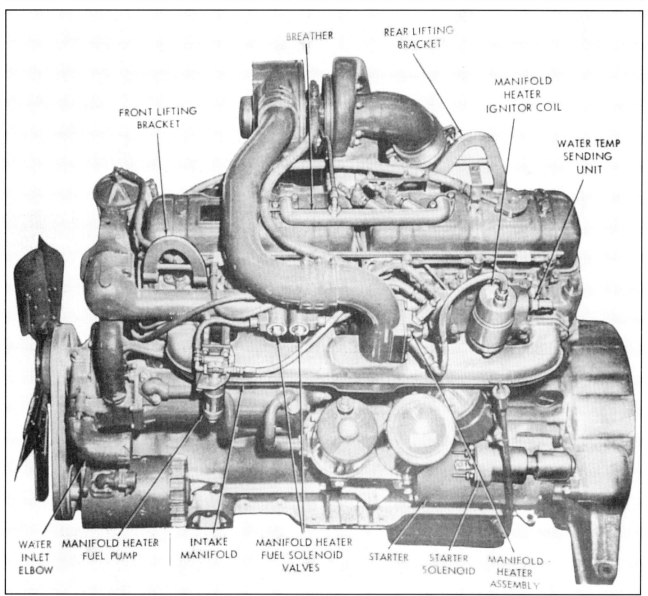

WATER
INLET
ELBOW

MANIFOLD HEATER
FUEL PUMP

INTAKE
MANIFOLD

MANIFOLD HEATER
FUEL SOLENOID
VALVES

STARTER

STARTER
SOLENOID

MANIFOLD
HEATER
ASSEMBLY

FRONT LIFTING
BRACKET

BREATHER

REAR LIFTING
BRACKET

MANIFOLD
HEATER
IGNITOR COIL

WATER TEMP
SENDING
UNIT

Mack M123   Truck, 10-ton, 6x6, Tractor, M123   1955

GENERAL

During 1952-69 Mack built 8,782 M-series tactical 5- and 10-ton 6x6 trucks of which the M123 and M125 were the most imposing. Mack began building these 10-tonners in 1955 with V8 petrol/gasoline engine but for improved cruising range a diesel engine (Cummins V8) was introduced for the M123 with a model designation change to M123A1. Existing trucks were re-engined and known as M123E1 (these were in the s/n range M123M1001 to 1157 and probably beyond). The USMC also had some and a small quantity was exported, e.g. to Australia. In the 1960s Consolidated Diesel Electric Co., a Division of Condec Corp., became the prime contractor, with Mack supplying the axles and transmissions.

PHYSICAL

Large conventional tractor truck with soft-top cab (as on 5-ton model, *qv*). Variants: M123C had single (vs dual) midship winch and low-mounted fifth wheel coupling; M123D had dual midship winches again and low-mounted fifth-wheel; M123A1C had diesel engine and single rear winch. Wheelbase was 181.5 in., BC 60 in. Overall dimensions 280 x 114 x 113 (min. 91) in. Weight 30,230 lb.

TECHNICAL

LeRoi T-H844 V8-cyl. 844-cid ohv petrol engine, producing 297 bhp (gross) at 2,600 rpm. Mack TRDXT72 5F1R gearbox, 2-speed transfer. Mack triple-ratio front axle, dual-ratio rear axles, all 9.02:1. Air brakes. Power-assisted steering. Tyres 14.00-24. 12/24-V electrics. Dual 45,000-lb winches.

Top and *above:* M123 with high fifth wheel and dual winches.

Below: Early model being demonstrated on a steep incline.

The M123 was used primarily for tank hauling. One is seen here with 45-ton tank-transporter semi-trailer M15A1 and as such it superseded the M26(A1) Pacific 'Dragon Wagon'. The tank is a T48 Medium. Note 1939/40 Dodge 1½-ton 4x4-based power drill.

Front axle steer/drive end and M123 with 19.50-21 rear tyres for use with experimental Trackporter, shown with M60 in June 1963.

Mack M125   Truck, 10-ton, 6x6, Cargo, M125   1955

GENERAL

In addition to the M123 tractors, several other variants were planned but only the M125 cargo/prime mover reached the production stage, albeit in small numbers. The pilot models were known as XM125 (1953-54). The chassis designation was M121 and the prime mover version was intended primarily for towing the 155-mm gun and 8-in. howitzer, in which respect it took on where the 1940s' Mack NO had left off. The M125 had a single winch, behind the front bumper. An experimental variant with Allison automatic transmission, the XM125E1, was built for tests and evaluation but not proceeded with; it had been intended for operation with the 175-mm gun. A dump truck was another project, but never appeared. Although the M125 was used mainly by the US Army, stateside and overseas, some found their way to Greece and possibly other NATO member countries.

PHYSICAL

Like the M123 (qv) but with a 14-ft steel cargo body with folding troop seats, bows and canvas cover. Wheelbase 181.5 in., BC 60 in. Overall dimensions 331 x 114 x 129 (min. 90) in. Weight 31,600 lb, GVW 51,000 (on highway 61,600) lb.

TECHNICAL

ngine, gearbox-cum-transfer case, axles, steering, wheels and tyres all same as M123 tractor version. Gar Wood DSA716 45,000-lb capacity winch, with 300-ft rope, at front. Chain hoist at rear. Max. road speed 42.5 mph. M125A1 had diesel engine.

Top: M125 under test. 550-odd would be built, during 1957-58.

Above: 5B1509 on display in Japan.

Below: Long-wheelbase closed-cab conversion for dynamometer use at Ft Belvoir, as seen in 1983.

Mack DM6116ST   Truck, 15-ton, 6x6, Tractor   1968

GENERAL

In 1968 Mack was awarded a contract for a batch of heavy-duty 6x6 chassis for the US Air Force. The majority were equipped with a fifth-wheel coupling and a winch behind the cab. These tractors were intended for use in conjunction with various types of semi-trailers, moving Rapid Runway Repair ('Triple R') equipment and other machinery. Mack DM600-series tractor trucks could be seen at USAF bases around the world, from Japan and Vietnam to Europe and back home, usually in USAF blue but also in olive drab. GVW and GCW ratings were 51,000 and 120,000 lb resp. The chassis was also used with a 7-yd dump body, again for airstrip and other construction and repair work on airfields.

PHYSICAL

Basically a commercial truck, with typical Mack DM-series off-set cab for better driver's visibility in both directions. Tall as a result of the driven front axle and unusual in having 'super single' tyres all round. All had the optional steel butterfly bonnet and swing-up front wings. Some had high-mounted headlamps and different bumper.

TECHNICAL

Own Maxidyne END673E 672-cid 180-bhp (net) 6-cyl. diesel engine and TRQ7220 18-speed Quadruplex transmission, driving rear or all wheels. Air-actuated brakes. Tyre size 18.00-22.5.

Top: New tractor (USAF 68B11031) as delivered in 1968.

Above: 69B2557 in the UK, 1981 (819th Red Horse squadron). Notice alternative headlamps location.

Below: Dump truck on DM6116S chassis (without winch), 1968.

Mack RM6866RS   Truck, 8-ton, 6x6, Cargo   1982

GENERAL

Following tests by the Australian Army during 1979-81
Mack Trucks Australia Pty Ltd received a contract for 940
eight-tonne trucks, with deliveries to begin in 1982.
Various body configurations were specified, most of
which are shown. (Not included are special-purpose
types like the bridging truck - for launching and
recovering Ribbon bridge sections -, the concrete mixer
and the bitumen distributor, the latter being the only
model not to have a driven front axle.) It would appear
that eventually just over 900 entered service. The base
vehicle is known as the Truck, Cargo, Heavy, MC3, with a
GS body by Walsh Engineering. Some were fitted with a
hydraulic loading crane, with outriggers, between cab
and body. Certain trucks were later retrofitted with
airbag rear suspension.

PHYSICAL

Typical Mack RM600-series in general appearance, but
with right-hand drive. Centre-mounted cab. Set-back
front axle. Dropside cargo GS body, 224 x 94 in. inside,
with bows and canvas cover. Wheelbase 215 in., BC
55 in. Overall dimensions 378 x 98 x 124 in. Weight
25,500 lb.

TECHNICAL

Own EM6-285 Maxidyne turbocharged 6-in-line diesel,
developing 285 bhp at 1,800 rpm. Maxitorque TRL1078
5F1R direct-top gearbox with TC150 2-speed transfer.
Full-time all-wheel drive. Own SS441C tandem bogie
with power divider. Fabco (Kelsey Hayes) SDA18B front
axle. Tyre size 12.00-20. Winch (10-ton Ateco 24L)
optional.

Top and *above:* The base vehicle is the Heavy Cargo GS, with
or without winch.

Below: Cargo truck with side boards and superstructure
removed.

The Abbey CTM3000 loading crane is a useful addition; it lifts maximum 7,500 lb at 6 ft radius. Body length is reduced by 18 in.

Aussie Macks are frequently used for long-distance work with one or two trailers carrying containers, AFVs and other loads.

Dump truck (capacity 8 cu.m.) and artillery tractor with crew shelter and ammo handling crane. Notice winch cable rollers at front.

The wrecker has Holmes A750 recovery gear and special equipment. Tankers are 11 400-litre refueller (left) and water distributor.

Mack RD8226SX   Truck, Tractor, 6x6   1986

GENERAL

In the mid-1980s Mack offered a special range of
militarized commercial 6x4 and 6x6 trucks (as
exemplified by the Australian job). Mack used the slogan
'An Army is only as efficient as its transport' and claimed
that 'the United States, Nigeria, Australia, Israel and
many other countries are using Mack trucks for heavy-
duty tactical operations'. The RD8226SX was presented
as ideal for tank transporters. It featured full-time all-
wheel drive and a wide range of options was offered to
suit varying requirements, e.g. an additional
compartment to accommodate tank crew members. Also
labeled 'The extra-strength truck', RD models were
available with a choice of more than 15 different
engines.

PHYSICAL

Typical Big Mack appearance with flat front, steel
butterfly hood with large sloping side panels, swing-up
flat-top steel mudguards, central-mounted 3-seat cab
with heavy winching gear behind. Wheelbase 227 (BC
55) in. Overall dimensions 333 x 103 x 145 in. GVW,
102,750 lb, GCW 202,960 lb.

TECHNICAL

Own Econodyne EE9 V8-cyl. 500-bhp turbocharged
diesel engine with inter-cooling. T2100 10-speed gearbox
and TC152 2-speed transfer case with inter-axle
differential. Air/hydraulic disc brakes at front, full-air
cam-type at rear. Tyres 12.00-24.

Top and *above:* Proposed tank transporter with matching semi-
trailer.

Below: Similar 6x6 tractor, Model RD8866 (with 285-bhp
ENDT676 engine) for the US Navy, registered 96-39079,
1983/84.

Some typical examples of heavy-duty six-by-six Macks for military service. *Above:* RD8006 of 1987/88 with right-hand drive for use by US Army in Japan and Pacific (colour: semi-gloss olive green with black chassis and grille). *Below:* RD8006 tractor for USAF, 1985 (colour: dark blue, black chassis). '00' in model designation was used if engine model code not known or specified.

Above and *below:* RM600-series 6x6 tractors for tank-transporter/HET semi-trailers, with crew cab, in South Africa in the late 1970s/early '80s. The RM models had full-time all-wheel drive with centre differential and torque proportioning. The photograph above right was taken during a parade of hundreds of military vehicles, aircraft and about 10,000 troops in Durban in late 1981. The 5-axle trailer was probably of indigenous manufacture; it carries a Centurion tank as it passes the City Hall.

Above: In the late 1980s the Israeli Defence Force (IDF) undertook extensive tank unit deployment tests. Prototype tractors by Autocar, Mack, MAN/ÖAF and Mercedes-Benz with semi-trailers from Agam and Netzer Sireni participated. Principal load was the 60-ton-plus Merkava tank. The Mack — an RD8886 6x6 — was not adopted and in due course migrated via Antwerp to Singapore.

Right: RM600SX prime mover built to meet the requirements of an undisclosed country.

Below: The early-1970s' F897ST 25-ton 6x4 seen on page 108 also appeared as a 6x6 prototype, designated F8976SX. Like the 6x4 it had dual winches, good for 30-ton pulls. The wheels were now of the disc-type. It remained an experiment.

Above: An RM600-series 6x6 wrecker with Holmes gear and crew cabin of the South African Defence Force (left) and an RM6866SX 40-ton single-jib wrecker built up by Century Wrecker Corp. of Ooltewah, Tennessee, in 1986. It rides on wide-base 24.00-21 single tyres and has a front winch. 'For an overseas military entity'.

Right and *below:* RM6006SX 6x6 chassis with Holmes twin-boom recovery equipment of the late 1970s. RM models had a conventional centre-mounted cab and all-wheel drive. The 6 indicated the model/series, the next two digits identified the engine (if known), the digit 6 was added for 6x6 and suffix SX indicated the chassis type, here an on/off-road six-wheeler.

Mack MB3   Truck, 8x8, Fire/Crash   1959

GENERAL

In the late 1950s a revolutionary fire/crash truck was
designed for the US Air Force and prototyped by Mack.
Going by detail differences on surviving photographs
two or possibly three were built, although one may have
been reworked. Intended for rapid deployment in case of
aircraft crashes off the beaten track the vehicle was a
marvel of high-mobility chassis engineering but may
have proved an overkill in terms of complexity and cost.

PHYSICAL

Eight-wheeled forward-control design with large cab,
swing-away foam nozzle at front and what looked like an
MG ring mount on top. The latter contained coiled
lengths of hose which could be pulled out for use on
both sides. The wheelbase was 128 in (between the
tandem axle bogie centres). Overall the rig measured
265 x 96 x 122 in. GVW was 21,435 lb.

TECHNICAL

Rear-mounted liquid-cooled V8 engine with twin
carburettors. Drive line comprised automatic
transmission, central transfer case and two differentials,
one in the centre of each bogie, from which the wheels
were driven by individual prop shafts in an X pattern.
The final drive was via spur gears concentric with the
king pins but only the four front wheels were steered. On
the sides of the diffs were extensions with hydraulic
drum brakes. All wheels were suspended independently,
with torsion-bar springing. Tyre size 9.00-20.

Top and *above:* The final prototype, seen in mid-1960.

Bottom: An earlier photograph, taken in July 1959.

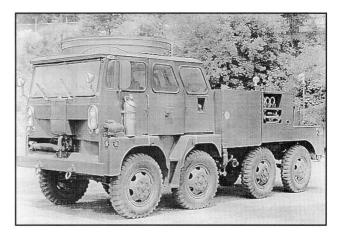

126

Side view and rare pictures of the undercarriage: front and rear suspension, central power divider/transfer case and rear bogie.

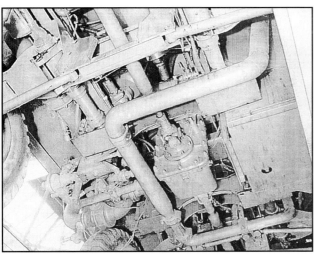

DA/Mack   Tractors, 25-ton, 8x8, XM376-377   1957

GENERAL

Officially known as Truck, Tractor, 25-ton, 8x8, XM376, with Gooseneck, and ditto XM377, these 8x8s were the front and rear components of the huge experimental 85-ft long Transporter, Tank, 50-ton, Double Ended, XM376, XM2, XM377, the middle unit being the connecting load platform suitable for carrying 50- to 60-ton payloads. The combination had a GVW rating of 228,040 lb. Two were assembled by Ordnance engineers at Detroit Arsenal - in 1956/57 - and Mack's contributions were the complete tandem bogies and axle sets: two elevated steering ones with triple reduction and two double-reduction rear axles for each tractor. It was another automotive phenomenon and just about the ultimate in US MV design of the era. Alas, it was also an overkill and not practical: in 1960 the vehicles were declared surplus.

PHYSICAL

Double-ended combination comprising load deck between front and rear units. Wheelbase of units 140 in., bogie centres 69 in. each, length 305 in. (rear unit 325 in.), width 114 in. Combination overall 1,021 x 116 x 133 in. Weight 128,040 lb.

TECHNICAL

(Each unit) Continental AOI-1195-1 8-cyl. air-cooled 560-bhp (gross) petrol engine with Allison CBT5640-2X 4F2R automatic transmission. Mack reduction box (2.00:1) and axles (9.02:1). Air brakes. Leaf-spring suspension. Ross steering, power-assisted. 18.00-25 tyres. Carco 30-ton winch.

Top and *above:* Combination complete; XM376 (USA 5B1060) at front, XM377 (USA 5B1062) at rear.

Below: XM377 (USA 5B1062) showing gooseneck.

For real-life use the rigs were totally impractical and as they were affected with technical problems the project was terminated.

Surplus: Army Macks in mufti

At the end of WWI many US Army Mack 3½- and 5-tonners stayed behind in French dumps, to be auctioned and transferred to civilian operators. The Bulldog below left was snapped in France as late as 1945, gas producer and all, and those on the right went to Denmark where they served until the 1960s (on pneumatic tyres since 1930). At least one survives (see page 154).

After 1945 again, numerous Macks went to work in Civvy Street. The EH types were liked because they were 'nearly civilian' although the engine was often replaced with a diesel (*bottom: Henschel-engined left,* Deutz *right*).

Opposite page: More EHs, some hardly recognisable as such, in Australia, Britain and Holland. The Briton — designated Mack H9T-162 — was reworked by Mack Trucks (GB) Ltd of North Street, Barking, Essex, in 1956. It had a Leyland diesel engine and Bedford cab. The firm also put several other configurations together from Mack and other parts, including a 4x4 COE using a Commer cab, but its main business was maintaining ex-WD Macks and supplying parts for these.

Top: Abandoned after hard civvy use but shown here because they are so rare: the bones of a 1942 FG in the Australian outback in 1990 and an NJU 4x4 in a French forest, both dieselized.

Above, left and *below:* Most LMSWs when demobbed continued their job as heavy recovery vehicles. Shown are two of the single-jib type (Billy Smart's Circus and a surviving Belgian example), the others being the twin-boom Canadian type, which were much in demand. British, Belgian and Dutch specimens are presented, with various degrees of transformation. Several such wreckers are still operational today and are likely to survive in one form or another.

A couple of LMSWs, recabbed and otherwise modified almost beyond recognition, in Holland and Germany many years ago.

Ex-WD EXBX diesel trucks were eminently suitable for extended use by civil engineering contractors, like KYH135 (London, 1950).

Willment's KYH135 slightly changed and a 1947-registered EXBX-2 of a Dorset showman, shortened and carrying a generating set.

In Holland many NR-series Macks were extensively reworked to meet users' demands. The Lanova diesel was advantageous.

Most conversions with single rear axle were used for tractor units hauling general cargo and liquids, usually on long-distance.

Above: Civilianized NRs on both sides of the Atlantic. Most were originally built with soft-top cab, so an enclosure or a new one was usually installed. The Austrian one (right) retains its military body.

Right: For European long-distance haulage the rejuvenated Macks invariably towed a suitable 2- or 3-axle trailer of the drawbar type, like this Dutch example with its stylish wide and elaborate new cab.

Below: German conversions in the 1950s, one (left) with Deutz F8L614 air-cooled Deutz diesel engine and very neat bodywork, the other, a 'reefer' from Hamburg retaining its nearly original nose.

Bottom: Two more Deutz diesel-engined NRs with totally changed appearance, in Germany (left) and Holland (c. 1958).

Many NRs were used for construction work: tippers, dumpers, tankers. These examples operated in Austria (left) and Australia.

The modernized Dutch trio has new Mack cabs. Below are a Dutch dumper and a French Geneve Super-Triplex 3-way tipper.

Top: Asphalt distributor with trailer in Holland in the 1950s and a similar outfit still operational in Belgium in the late 1980s, here at work at Braine-le-Comte.

Above: Belgian tanker combination of the Camerman firm in Antwerp, with Henschel engine and sheet metal transplant and (right) one in Australia in 1983, watering the Hume Highway Albury-Wodonga bypass, with Cummins engine and Leyland radiator.

Left: Dutch transformation with DAF diesel, Atlas crane, pole trailer. Cab and front wings have also been changed.

Below: Hardly recognisable as Mack NRs these metamorphosed examples feature full forward control and attractively styled bus and van bodywork, in Belgium and the Netherlands respectively, back in the 1950s.

Mack NR chassis with cranes: a revolving type in Austria and a simple derrick in Canada (1988), the latter with post-war Mack cab.

British recovery vehicle on shortened NR chassis with ex-FWD SU-COE cab and right-hand drive. Smethwick 1953 registration.

NR-14 as crane carrier in Malta (1993) and one of two Tracteur cranes (bodied by Beaufrère) once built for the Paris fire brigade.

The wartime Mack NM-series trucks with their six-wheel drive and big petrol engine were less suitable for civilian road haulage than the NR 6x4 diesel. In the early post-war years several did enter civil service, however; some converted to diesel (by transplant) and with their front-axle drive disconnected, but they were more useful for specialist roles where all-wheel drive was an important asset and petrol consumption less of a problem. Shown above are a few load carriers in Holland, with civvy bodies. The one on the left has a coachbuilt cab and wheelbase extension, the others look as if they have ended their second lease of life and destined to be dismantled for spares.

Left: Impressive German-bodied combination, also from the early post-WWII era. It carries a Hamburg registration. In Germany it was not unusual for the EY petrol engines to be modified to diesel operation, cleverly using Lanova parts and a Bosch fuel injection pump, as shown.

Below: Heavy road tractors with ballast: an Austrian unit from Vienna, left (notice the winch capstan head remaining in its original location) and on the right a UK job, also with extended cab, used by the British Testing Unit in Hendon, with an HYR registration like many of the Government-operated gritters and snowploughs (*qv*).

Relatively rare NM-based tractor unit for semi-trailers, hauling a weighty Ohrenstein & Koppel (O&K) crawler crane in Holland.

Unusual 2-axle conversion used as a tractor for Netam low-loader, also in Holland. Cab roof looks like ex-CMP; not uncommon.

Another imposing transformation in post-war Germany, with 'night cab' and tandem-axle semi-trailer by Blumhardt of Wuppertal.

With its sturdy off-road chassis construction the NM was an excellent candidate for dump trucks, here in Germany and Holland.

Sporting a new Netam 3-way tipper, simple cab enclosure (with stock windscreen) and repaint this NM was ready for a new task.

Of all the ex-WD Macks in the UK the NM was the most numerous. Here are one rebuilt by Mack (GB) and another just rebodied.

Many showmen (circus and fairground operators) employed NM-series Macks, chiefly NM-5 and -6 (as surplussed from the British Army), for towing duties and/or as generator tractors. Here are some typical examples: FJU63 (with non-standard front wheels) worked with operator A. Holland and OHK65 with A. Downs of Chelmsford. JLV760 of J. P. Collins & Sons, seen in the two photographs above, doubled up as tractor and power source.

Left: The Dutch Circus Mikkenie had a nice fleet of Macks: at least three NMs and two LMSWs, all recabbed and rebodied.

Below: Billy Smart's Circus also had several. JXW2 is shown with generating set and with ex-LMSW crane and cab enclosure. (See *Wheels & Tracks* No. 63.)

The NM chassis was also well suited for heavy recovery vehicles. The crane was often transplanted. Here two Austrian examples.

Messrs Boekestijn of Maasland, near Rotterdam, used this wrecker with coachbuilt cab and heavy-duty single-jib recovery crane.

Gar Wood equipment with lengthened boom in Holland, still with folding top and one with exceptionally large cab in Scotland.

Some NMs served as undercarriages for cranes and draglines. On the left a Priestman on chassis with half-cab. Both in Holland.

Pair of water carriers of the French fire service. The one on the right has its complete nose replaced with a rather ugly substitute.

Two more Dutch conversions, seen in the 1970s and early '80s: a crane and a pile driver, the latter with substantial outriggers.

Of the British Army's Mack NMs many were transferred to the Ministry of Transport and County Council Highways Departments for use as bulk grit spreaders and snowploughs. Above are examples in Yorkshire and Lancashire, the latter in action after heavy snowfall. On the left is a reworked NM, a product of Mack Trucks (Great Britain) Ltd, which assembled 'Mack' trucks from American and British components. Truck shown was a 7-ton 6x6 with Perkins R6 diesel engine and rhd of 1960. Below it is possibly the same vehicle, seen in Scotland 28 years later and used by Grampian Regional Council, now as a recovery vehicle. Below right is a recabbed snowplough/gritter. At the bottom of the page we see an NM with Scania rhd forward-control cab and another snowplough, both stationed in Scotland again.

Back in the 1960s and '70s in Britain the Mack NO (7½-ton 6x6 in military parlance) was often called the Super Mack, and they were huge. In Civvy Street they found use for several purposes, from amusement (fair organ, left) to wreckers. The one on the right still worked in a Malta shipyard in 1997.

Some NOs were used for towing semi-trailers, usually low-loaders (Belgium, left; Japan, below left; France, below right). Above is an unusual single-rear axle conversion employed for timber haulage; it had a Deutz air-cooled diesel engine and was operated in Holland.

In Germany and the Netherlands — and no doubt elsewhere — certain NOs were converted to dumpers. Sometimes the winch was removed to save weight.

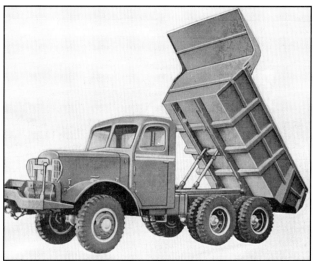

When the British Army surplussed its NOs in the late 1960s many were converted to wreckers, with a variety of cranes and cabs.

The Mack above and below left was worked hard and with only a stubby jib tackled the heaviest jobs. On the right a Holmes 600.

Typical wreckers in Belgium and Austria. The latter was extensively altered and belonged to the fire brigade of the City of Graz.

More wreckers, in France and back home in the USA (below). After demob many US MVs repatriated, for work or preservation.

THE 'MIGHTY-MACK'
MODEL N-O
TRUCK, PRIME MOVER, 7½ TON, 6 x 6, W/WINCH

SPECIFICATIONS

Weight (lb) .... Net 24,103
Live-axle gear ratio 9.02:1
Tires:
  Ply 14 Size 12.00x24; Pressure (psi)
                front 80; rear 65
  Tread, center-to-center, front
                   (in.) 76½

Vehicle dimensions:
  CA .... (in.) 82
  Cab to end of frame ....(in.) 141
  Wheel base .... (in.) 156
  OA length .... (in.) 296 3/4
  Ground clearance .... (in.) 12 9/16
  Loading height, empty .... (in.) 63¼
  Pintle height, loaded ..(in.) 42 5/8
  Body inside dimensions (in.):
    Length 132
    Width 96
    Height 58
  Body cargo space .... (cu ft) 425

Electrical system (volts) ..6; starting 12
  No. of batteries .... (6-volt) 2
  Type of ground .... positive

Brakes:
  Manufacturer; Bendix-
    Westinghouse .... Type, air
  Parking brake, type propeller-shaft

Transmission:
  Forward speeds 5
  Gear ratio .... High 1:1; Low 8:05:1

Transfer:
  Speeds 2
  Gear ratio ...High 1:1; Low 2:55:1

Capacities:
  Fuel .... (gal) 160
  Cooling system .... (qt) 54
  Crankcase, refill .... (qt) 19
  Transmission .... (qt) 14
  Transfer (w/PTO) .... (qt) 15
  Axles (qt) ....front 7 ½;
               rear (each) 11 ¼

Winch:
  Oil capacity (qt) 3
  Load capacity (lb) 45,000

PERFORMANCE
Computed grade ability in
lowest gear, loaded ....(percent) 65
Turning radius .... (ft.) 36
Fording depth .... (in.) 48
Cruising range, loaded .... (mi) 400
Allowable speed, governed ..(mph) 40

ENGINE
Manufacturer: Mack .... Model EY
  (New Cummins—HN230 Optional)
Type .... 4-cycle, valve-in-head;
    No. of cylinders (in line) 6
Displacement .... (cu in.) 707
Bore .... (in). 5
Stroke .... (in.) 6
Compression ratio 5.35:1
Governed speed .... (rpm) 2,100
Brake horsepower (max w/std
accessories) .... 159 at (rpm) 2,100
Torque (max w/std
accessories) .... 534 lb-ft at (rpm) 800

ADDITIONAL DATA
Live axles, type ......double-reduction,
             full-floating
Transmission, type ....constant-mesh

'Mighty Mack' back home following post-war military service in Europe, to be sold in the USA. It has a Belgian cab (see page 85).

Post-war M-series Mack and other 5-ton 6x6 trucks when demobbed have found civilian buyers but are usually modified quite extensively. Here Dutch (RAM) and Italian (Sirecome) conversions with 3-way and rear-tipping dump bodies and diesel engines.

French-operated M52 tractor with M127 semi-trailer. Below are a large van and one with new cab and Coles petrol-electric crane.

The 10-ton M-series was less suitable for civvy employment but a few made it, like these M123 tractor trucks, one in Japan, the other in Belgium. The latter (s/n M1070) has a Deutz V12 17.5-litre diesel engine, needing plenty of air to produce its 340 horses.

Still featuring Mack transmission and axles, later M123s were built by Condec. Here are some, demobbed, 'as-is' and refurbished.

Colourful Macks

In this colour supplement we present a selection of historic military Mack trucks which have been preserved for a variety of reasons by owners in several countries. Compared with commercial types these old soldiers are in the minority and it is remarkable that most

of the surviving military Macks are not in America but in Europe and Australia. Most MV events attract a Mack or two and they always draw much attention, a Mack being more than just a truck.

Many Macks having been sent across the Atlantic as military aid and their subsequent extended service life undoubtedly accounts for the relatively high survival rate in the 'old world' and

'down under' In books about Mack trucks the military models generally have not been given the attention they deserve and recent Mack sales promotion blurb claims that the company 'has been a supplier to the military since WWI'. See page 6 for when it really began, in 1911!

The pictures on this page are from a 1945 Mack calendar and display a certain amount of 'artistic licence' . . .

Rejuvenated Bulldogs from the WWI era: Mack ACs in Britain and Denmark, the latter modernized (in c.1930) to pneumatic tyres.

In the mid-1980s a 1916 AC was restored by Mack and European owner RVI for the Fondation de l'Automobile Marius Berliet.

WWII-vintage E-series Class 125 fire truck in the US of A and demilitarized (ex-S/M2765) EHT tractor truck rebuilt in Scotland.

Preserved in the Netherlands these LMSW wreckers were in civilian service for decades, the first with the Amsterdam Tramways.

Holland harbours several surviving LMSW wreckers but this is one of the few to have been restored to original military state.

Mack NRs, ex-Denmark and Italy respectively, now retired in Belgium. After 1945 few of these were used for military purposes.

Two rather unusual NRs: a civilianized Dutch 4x2 conversion and a timber hauler after 30 years of hard labour in South Australia.

Another NR in captivity 'down under', preserved in the livery it wore most of its life. The original open cab was retained, though.

NRs in civilian colours and OD: NR-13 with post-war cab in Holland and NR-14 in Belgium. Serials NR4D7442D and 15636D resp.

Preserved demilitarized NMs are rare but here are a recovery vehicle with Holmes crane and a typical snowplough pusher.

'The Strathie', a British reworked Mack NM from Strathpeffer, Scotland, with 1960 Aberdeen registration, closed cab and tipper.

Very rare early NM preserved in Sweden (w/closed cab; probably NM-2 with later hood) and an NM-5 or -6 converted in Canada.

Preserved NM-6 prime movers seen in France. Both look quite authentic and well restored. Mack built 7,236 NMs during 1940-45.

Normandy 1984 and a trio of Macks in Bayeux. From left: NO 7½-ton and NM 6-ton 6x6 from the UK and a Dutch NR 10-ton 6x4.

Before and after, but not the same truck! On the left a kept-to-be-rebuilt NM in Australia, the other a superb British renovation.

Of the big NO prime movers 2,050 were built during 1943-45. Here are restored examples of the breed from Belgium and Holland.

Most surviving NOs were 1950s' MDAP rebuilds with new steel body. This ex-British (BAOR) example resides in the Netherlands.

A fair number of NMs and NOs survive, several brought back to virtually authentic condition. Here two more NOs, both in the UK.

Post-war demobbed Mack tractor trucks on British rally fields: 1977 ex-USAF R611ST 6x4 (left) and 1950s' ex-US Army M123.

INDEX

American LaFrance	34, 78
Bernard	7
Brockway	7, 78
Century	125
Christie	18, 19
Condec, Condiesel, Consolidated	104, 152
Detroit Arsenal	128, 129
Diamond T	97, 110
Fontaine	160
Gar Wood	44, 46, 47
Holmes	100, 120, 125
International	110
Kenworth	78
Kovatch	104
Locomobile	9
Mack fire/crash trucks	34-36, 71, 78, 126, 127, 154
Mack half-tracks	96, 97
Mack semi-trailers (G578)	28-30
Mack truck models	
AB	6, 8-10
AC	6, 11-17, 130, 154
AP 6x4	17
B-series	102
CL713	160
DE	20, 23
DM-series	7, 100, 104, 106, 107, 117
E-series (EE-EH) (G624)	20-37, 130, 131, 154
EH mil. types (G533)	31-34
EXBX 6x4	49, 50
F-series (FC/G/K/P/T)	37, 38, 51, 68, 132
FG (G557)	38, 132
FPD (G640)	37
F897ST 6x4	108
F8976SX 6x6	124
Junior	6
L-series (LF/J/P)	39, 40, 44-48, 51, 66, 67, 99
LMSW 6x4 (G652)	44-47, 132, 133, 155
M15X, M20X	101
Mil. M-series	
5-ton, 6x6	110-113, 151
10-ton, 6x6	114-116, 152, 160
MB3	126, 127
MB410	101
MC400P	101
MR600S	108
MS-series Mid-Liner	101
NB 6x4 (G629)	43
ND, NH	33
NJU 4x4	41, 42, 132
NM-series 6x6 (G535)	7, 69-77, 132, 139-145, 157, 158
NN 6x6	71, 72
NO-series 6x6 (G532)	79-91, 146-150, 153, 158, 159
NQ 6x6	89-91, 153
NR-series 6x4 (G528)	52-65, 134-138, 153, 155, 156, 158
NW 6x6	67
R-series	100, 103, 105, 106, 118-125, 160
Senior	6
T3 Half-track	94, 95
T8, T8E1 Double-ender	92, 93
T9 Double-ender	93
T15, T16 6x6	89-91
T18, T19 Half-track	96, 97
T54 6x6	109
Traffic types	40
Ultra-Liner	108
XM376, 377 Double-ender	128, 129
RAM	151
RAMTA	106
Renault	7, 12, 101, 160
Reo	71
Roadless Traction	18, 19
Sirecome	151
Sterling	71
Tanks	
Cunningham	14
Ram	98
Renault	12
Sherman	98
Stuart	54
Tank transmissions, engines	7, 98, 160
White	9, 97

A glimpse into the future. . .

For tomorrow's tank-hauling needs Mack Trucks, in conjunction with trailer maker Fontaine Specialized, Inc., has designed the Military Transport Answer (MTA) concept: a Mack CL713 model tractor with customized trailer, claimed to be the only rig that can 'easily obtain permits to transport the 70-ton Abrams M1A2 tank over US highways and bridges in all 50 states'. It is available with Mack's 500-bhp 16.4-litre E9 V8 diesel, which parent company Renault V.I. offers in militarized form as a replacement AFV engine (e.g. for the French Army's AMX 30 B2 tank).

MACK TRUCKS' BASIC TRAINING IS THE TOUGHEST IN THE WORLD.

You get more than a fighting chance with Mack's range of Military Trucks. Because no other truck is built like a Mack Truck.

Its legend in toughness began in 1900 and grew through two World Wars. Whether on the battlefields of France or North Africa, Mack Trucks became legends in their own lifetimes. They still are.

Rugged, dependable and tenacious, they withstood the roughest terrain and took the toughest conditions in their stride, and always came back for more.

The legend shines on in the present range of Mack Military Trucks. What other truck has as many quality engineered parts and components built by its own company?

What other Military truck is more rugged? More durable? Tougher? It is part of Mack Trucks uncompromising commitment to producing one of the most impressive and sought after range of trucks in the world.

The Greatest Name in Trucks.

Inspect our range of military trucks and learn how Mack can complement your transportation arsenal.

Write to: Mack Trucks Inc., Mack International, Dept 3020, Allentown, Pennsylvania 18105, USA.

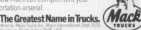

A LEGEND IN ITS LIFETIME. BECAUSE OF ITS LIFETIME.

Mack Trucks. Built for the needs of a world where you can't afford to stand still.

For detailed information on how custom-built heavy duty Mack trucks can be designed for your individual country requirements, contact a Mack distributor or write to: Mack Trucks, Inc., Mack International, Department M5, Allentown, Pennsylvania 18105, U.S.A. Telex: 847429. Cable: Mackworldwide.

The Greatest Name in Trucks

One of the Signal Companies.

An army is only as efficient as its transport.

Tank transporters, troop carriers, fuel carriers, dump trucks, tractors and wreckers are just as important to an army as the tanks and artillery.

And no-one makes defense transportation stronger or more reliable than Mack.

Mack trucks are built to survive in any climatic conditions, and over the most severe terrain, even in the hands of a non-professional driver.

That's because of the way a Mack truck is built — from the heavy duty chassis down to refined engine parts, components are engineered to tolerances of less than 15 ten thousandths of a millimeter (0.0015).

The high torque-rise engine requires fewer gear steps, which makes it easier to drive and more durable.

Mack trucks also have full time all wheel drive with high ground clearance yet low profile, to make them highly manoeuverable over rough terrain, while making you a smaller target.

In fact, so many features of a Mack truck are original, they have to be protected by Mack patents — the power train, for instance, with its unique constantly engaged transfer case gives a longer more durable life with fewer service intervals.

The Mack defense transportation range can be tailored to individual needs, but it is based on our range of commercial trucks, so parts are readily available and servicing is standardised.

You can rely on Mack to get you there — but more importantly get you back.

If you would like to know more about the Mack multi-purpose defense transportation range write to Mack Trucks, Inc, Department of International Defense Transportation, 2100 Mack Blvd, Allentown, Pennsylvania 18105 USA, Telex No. 847429.

The Greatest Name in Trucks.

armada 204

Is there an assault course a Mack can't cope with?

Mack trucks can be designed and built to operate anywhere from the frozen wastelands of the Antartic to the kiln-like temperatures of the Sahara.

A Mack can go from one extreme to the other because of the exceptional way in which it has been built.

The crankshaft, for instance, is engineered to a tolerance of less than ten 15 thousandths of a millimeter (0.0015).

Then there's the high torque-rise engine to consider — because it requires fewer gear steps, it's easier to drive and is more durable, especially in the hands of a non-professional driver.

Mack trucks also have full time all wheel drive with high ground clearance, yet low profile, to make them more manoeuvrable over rough terrain, while making you a smaller target.

In fact, so many features of a Mack truck are original, they have to be protected by Mack Patents — the power train, for instance, with its unique constantly engaged transfer case, gives a longer more durable life, with fewer service intervals.

The Mack range of tank transporters, troop carriers, water carriers, dump trucks, tractors and wreckers can be tailored to your individual needs.

But, they are based on our range of commercial trucks, so parts are readily available and servicing is standardised.

So if there's a load to be carried, be it a 70 ton tank or a fuel bowser, Mack build the trucks to do it.

After the testing we give a Mack truck, your assault course will look quite tame.

If you would like more information about the Mack multi-purpose defense transportation range, write to Mack Trucks, Inc, Department of International Defense Transportation, 2100 Mack Blvd, Allentown, Pennsylvania 18105 USA, Telex No. 847429.

The Greatest Name in Trucks.

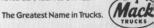